For my family:

You are everything.

I love you.

I generally avoid temptation unless I can't resist it.

- Mae West

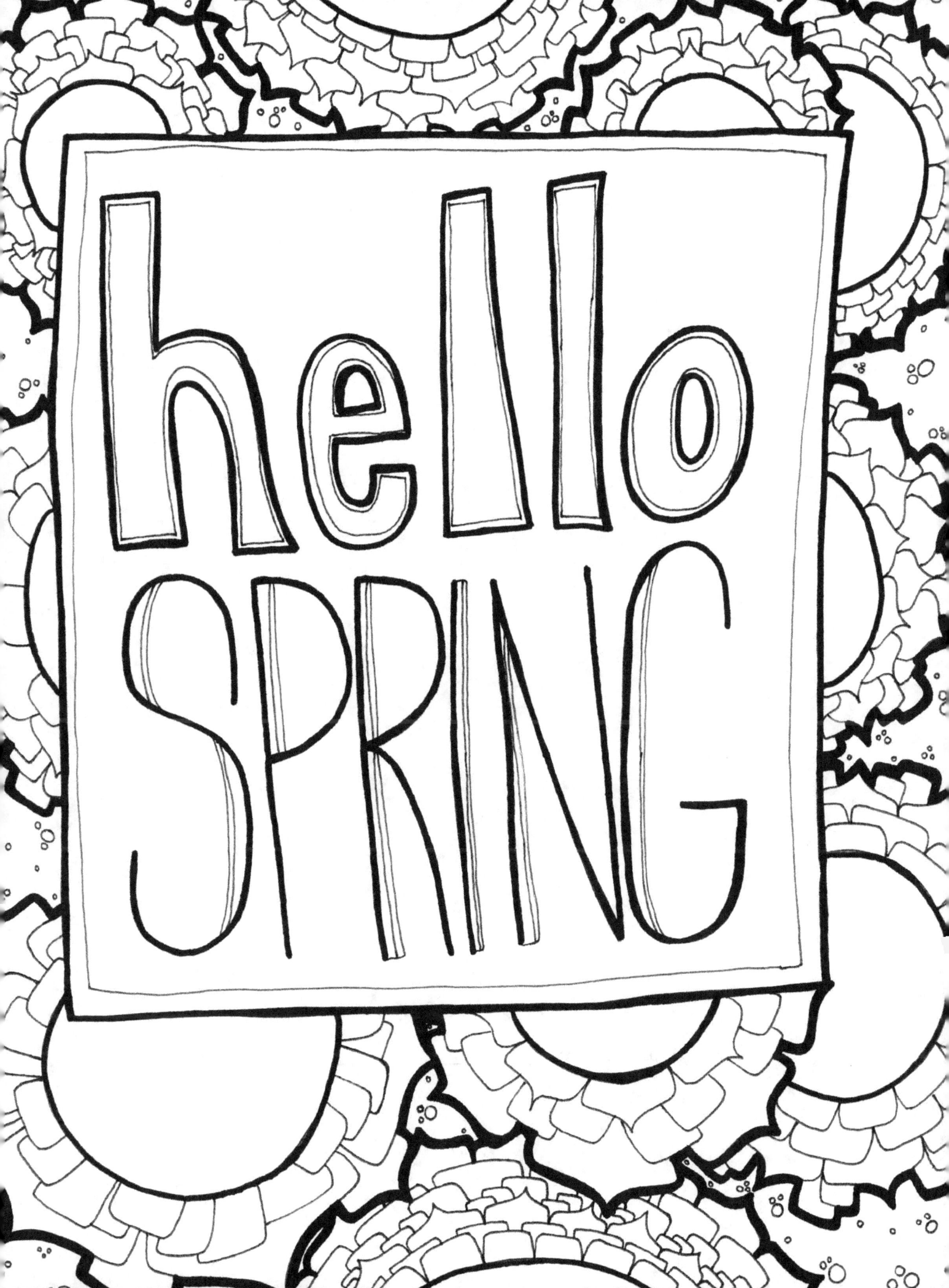

SarahMe Doodles Spring

Colored By: _____

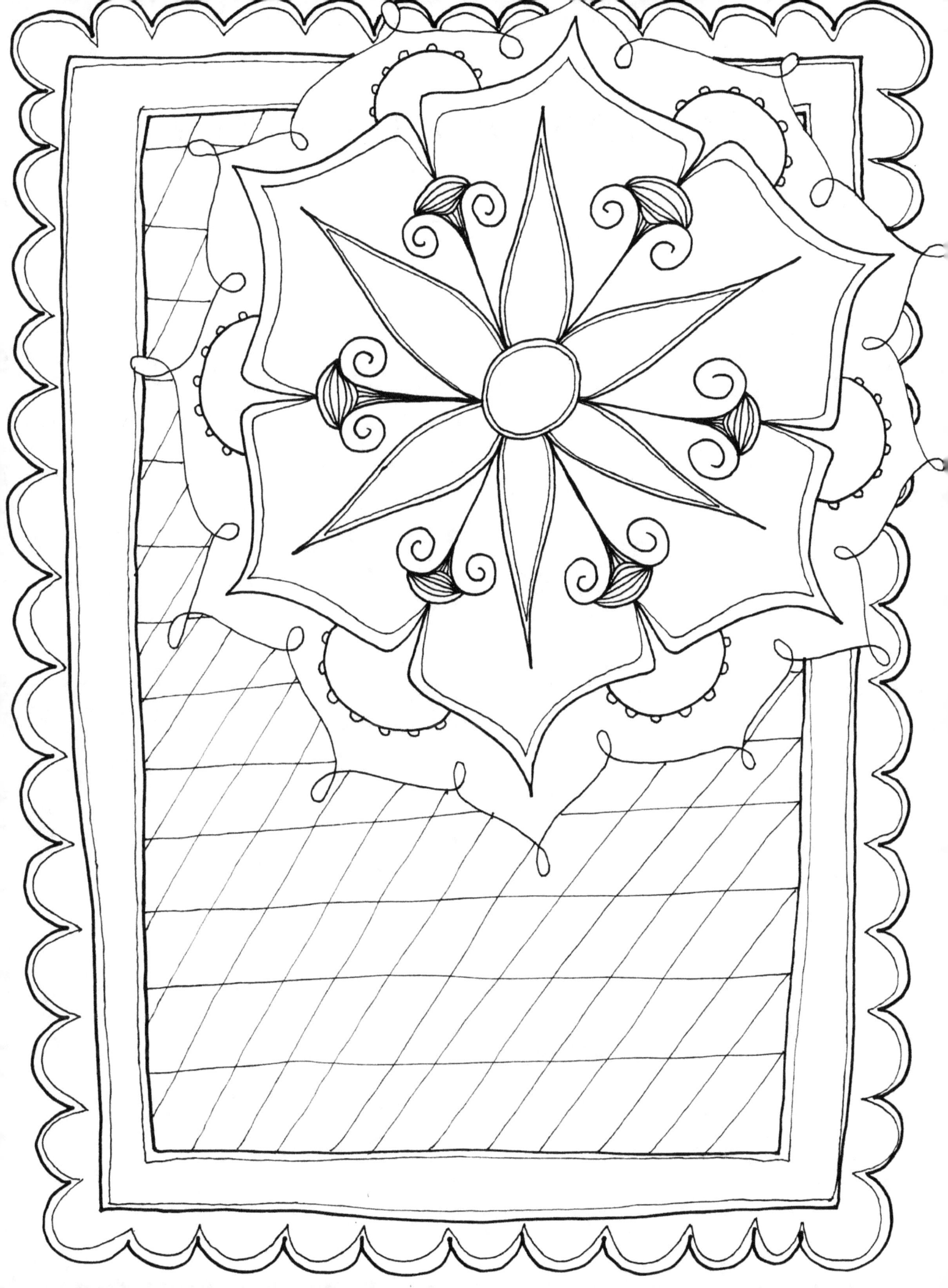

SarahMe Doodles Spring

Colored By: _____

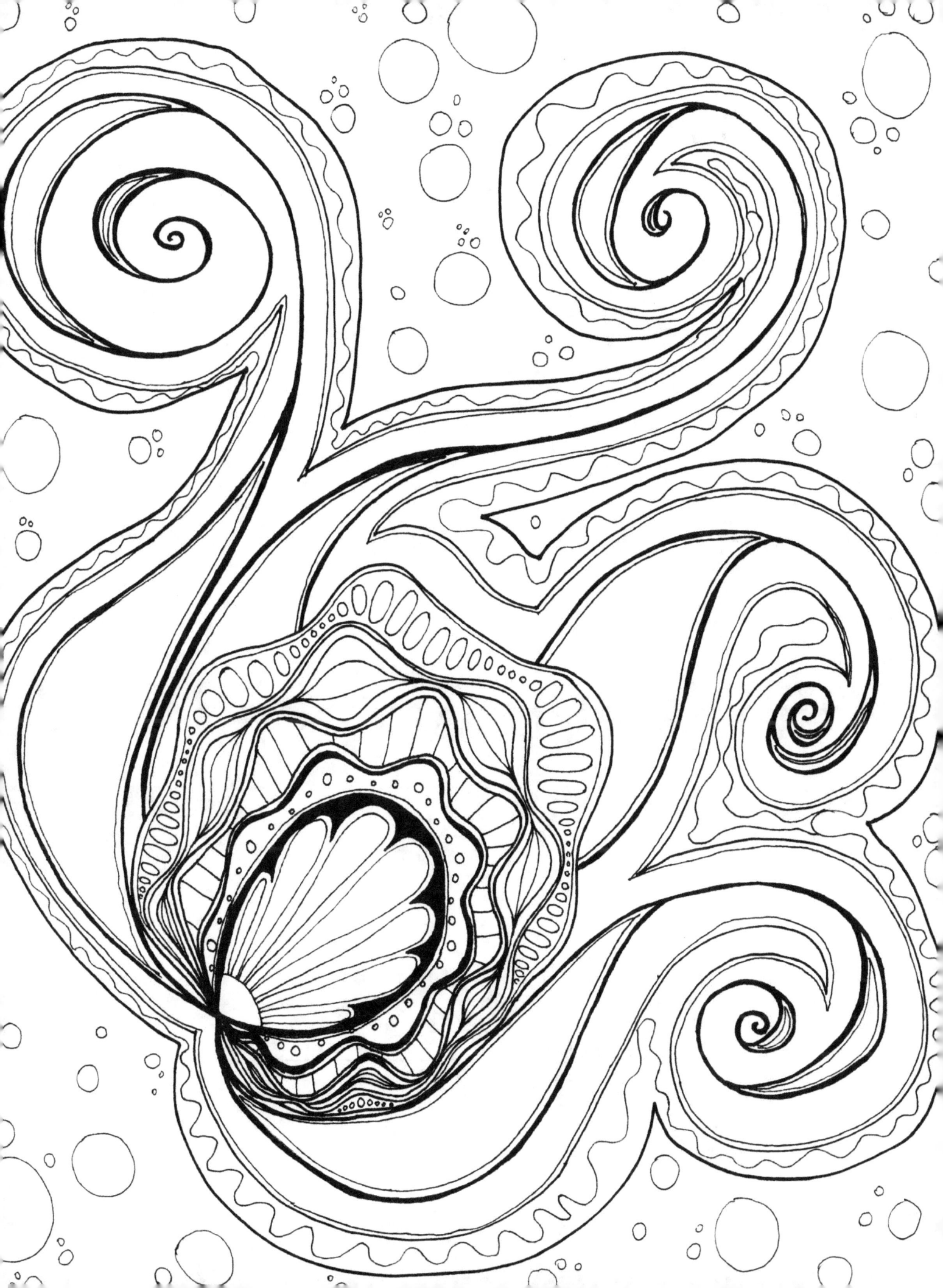

SarahMe Doodles Spring

Colored By: _____

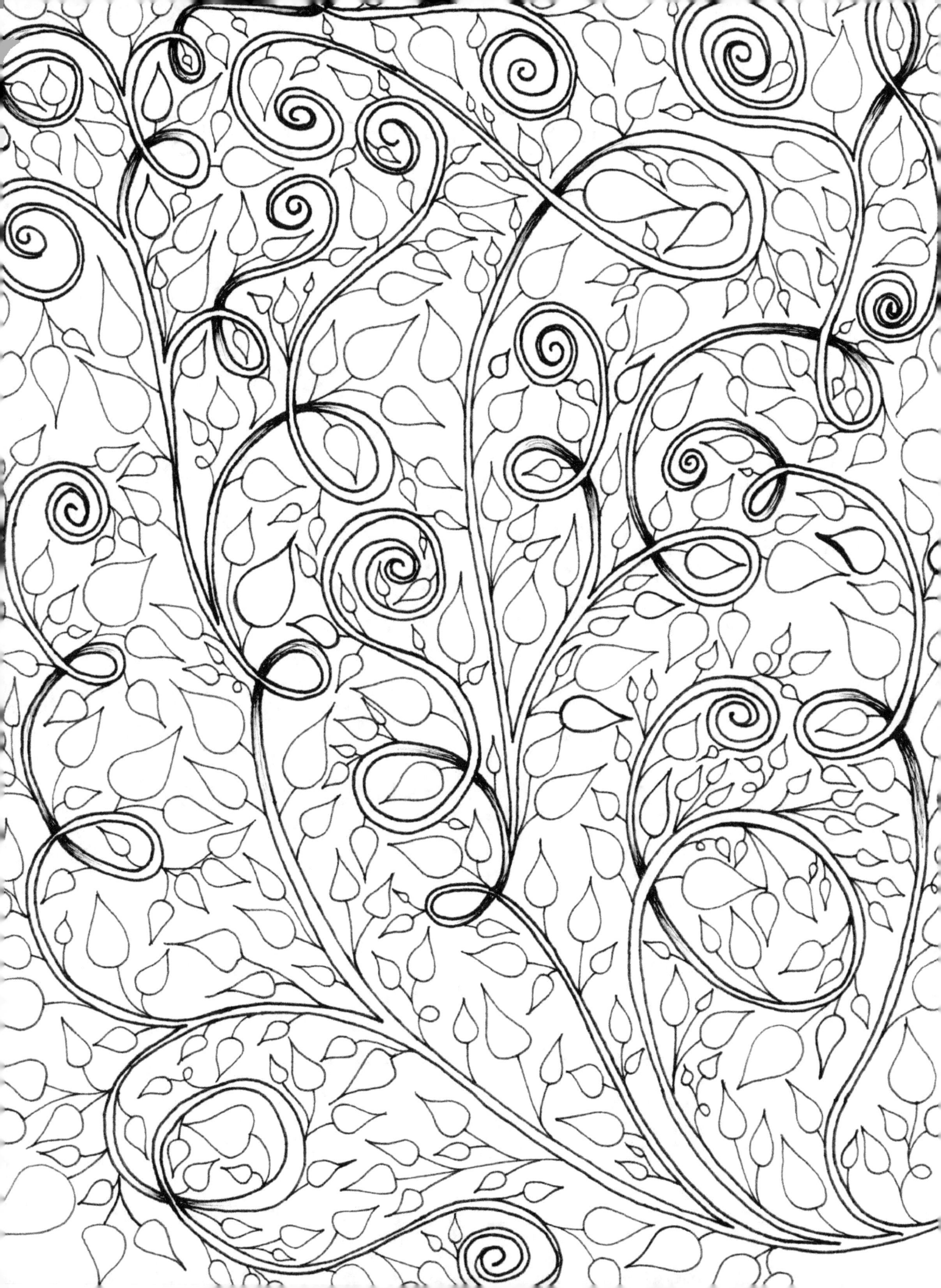

SarahMe Doodles Spring

Colored By: _____

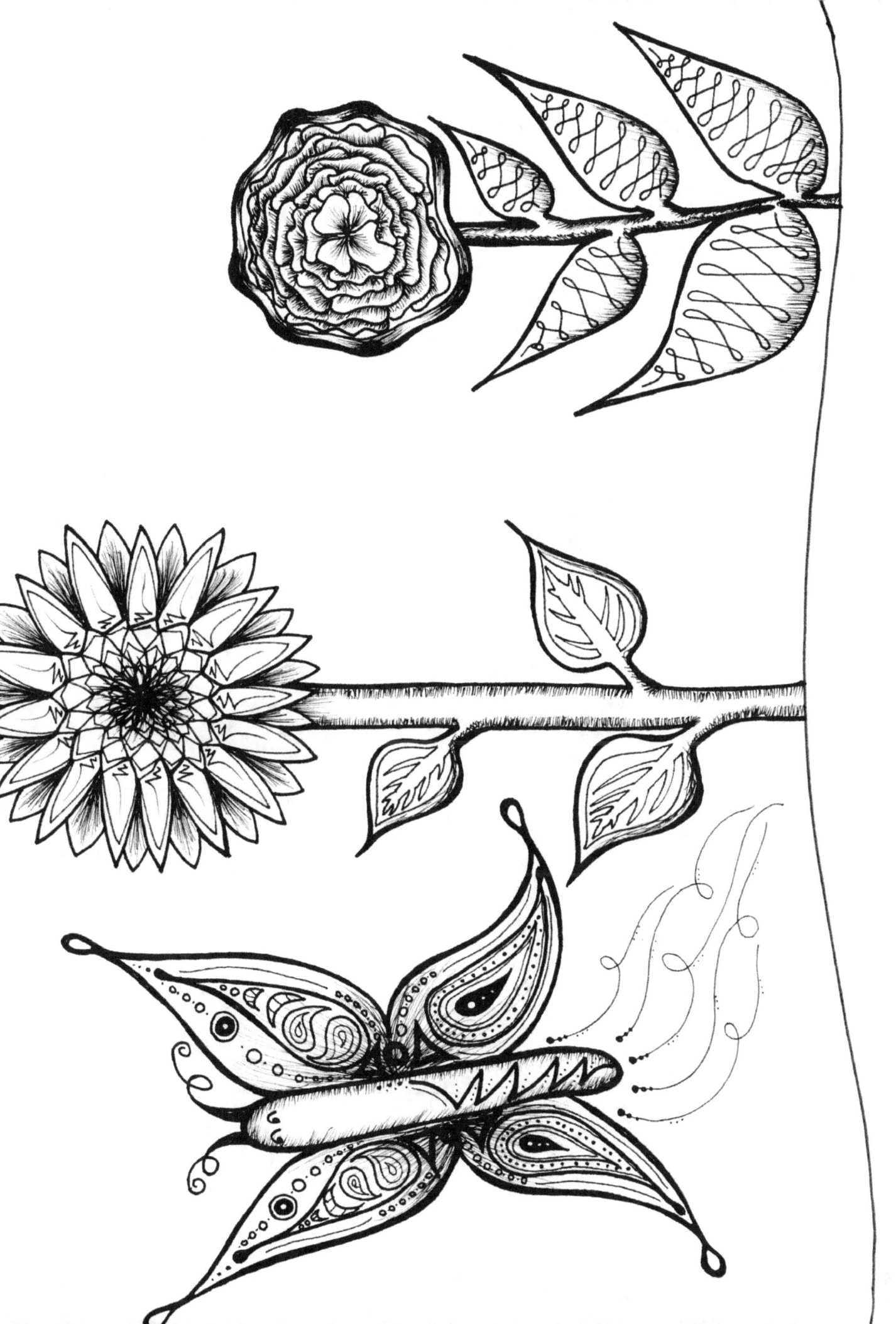

SarahMe Doodles Spring

Colored By: _____

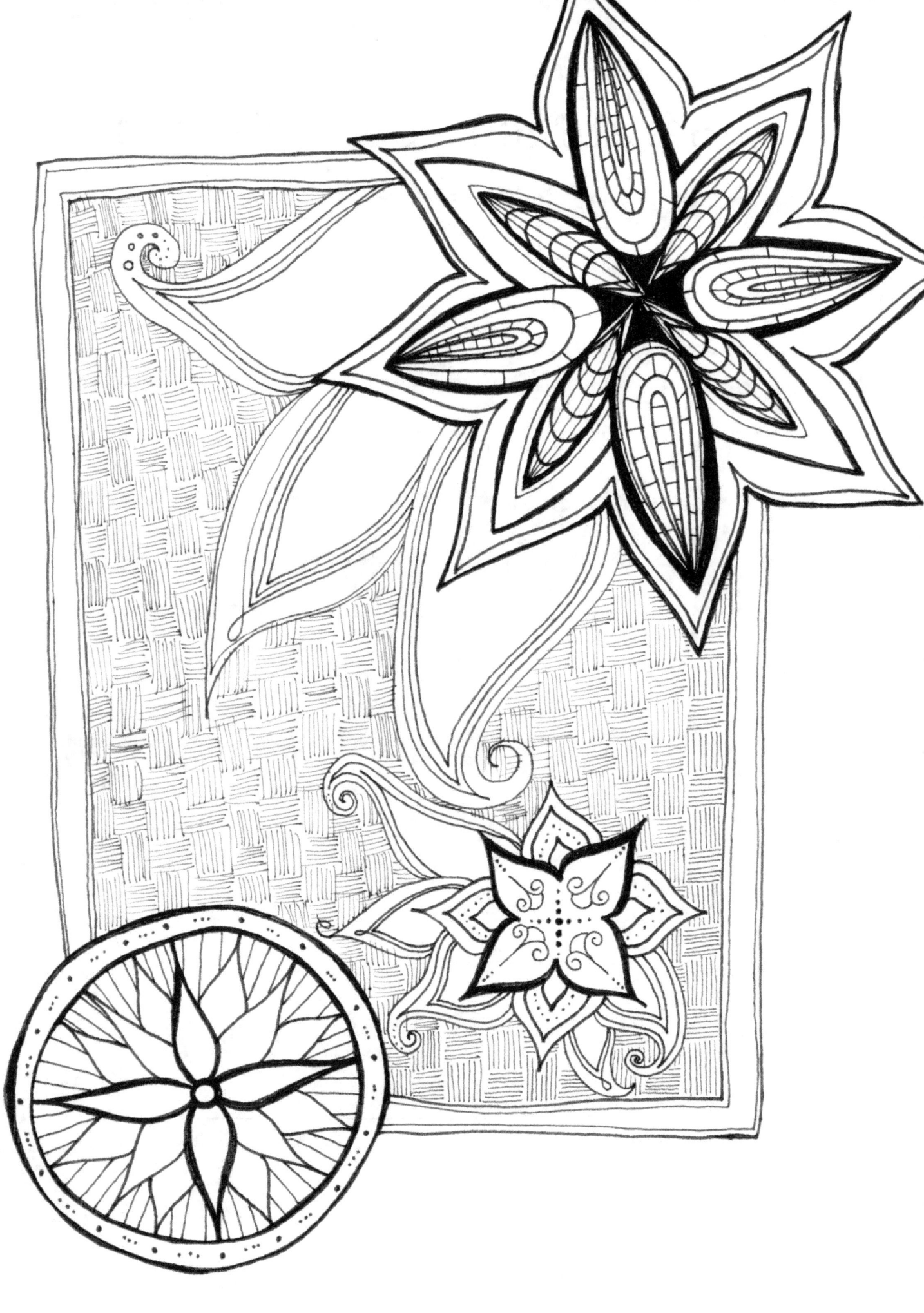

SarahMe Doodles Spring

Colored By: _____

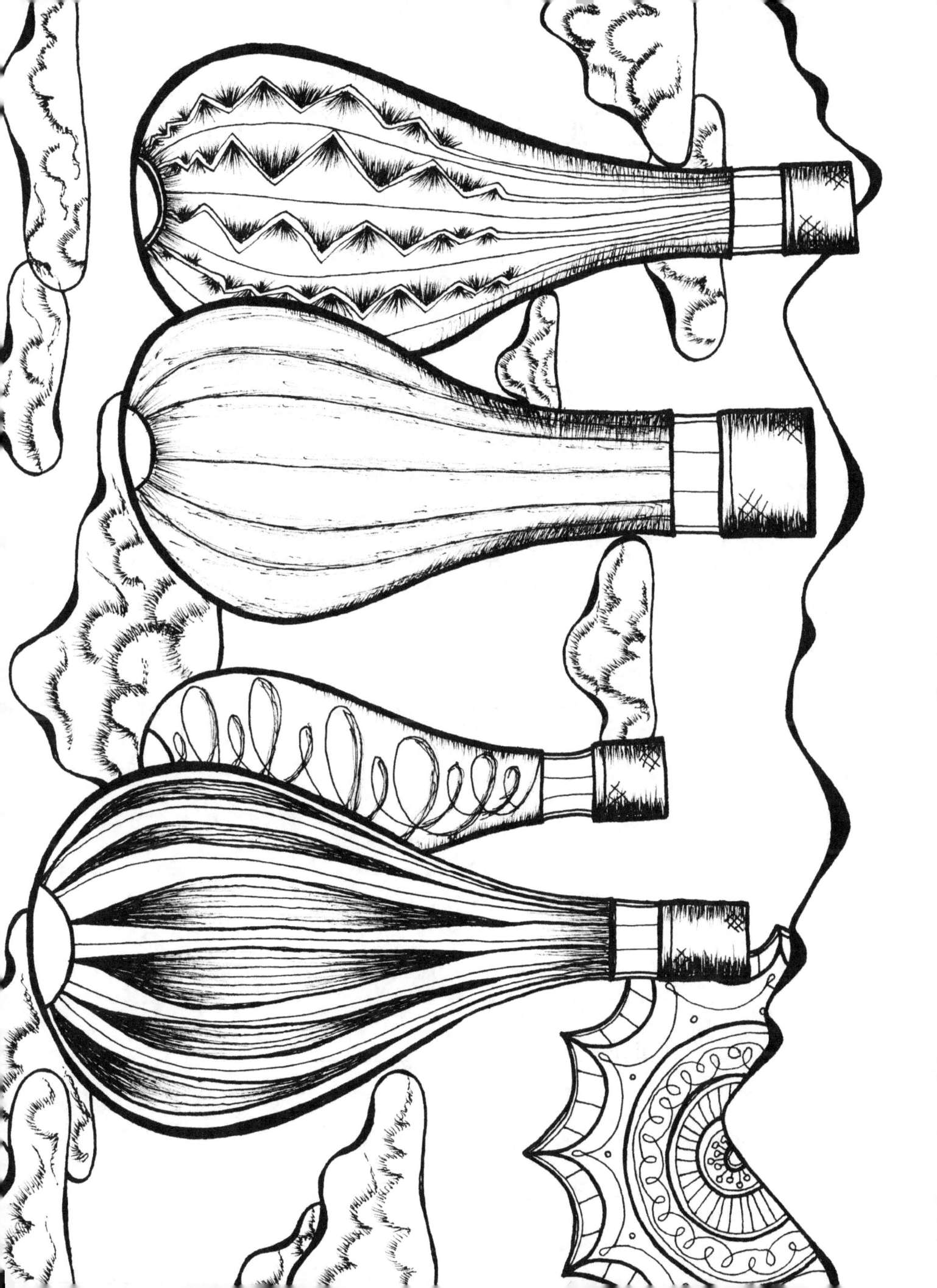

SarahMe Doodles Spring

Colored By: _____

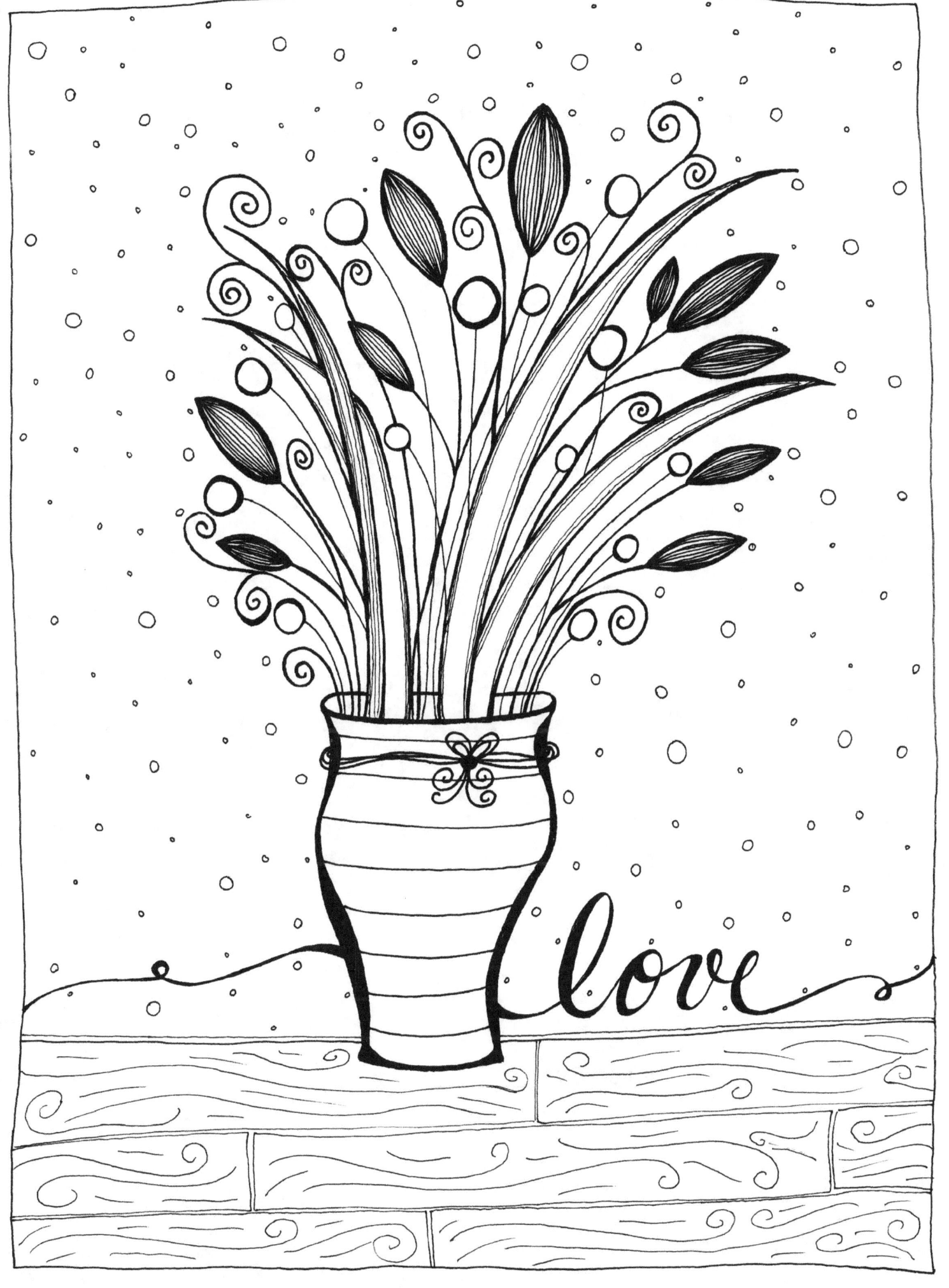

SarahMe Doodles Spring

Colored By: _____

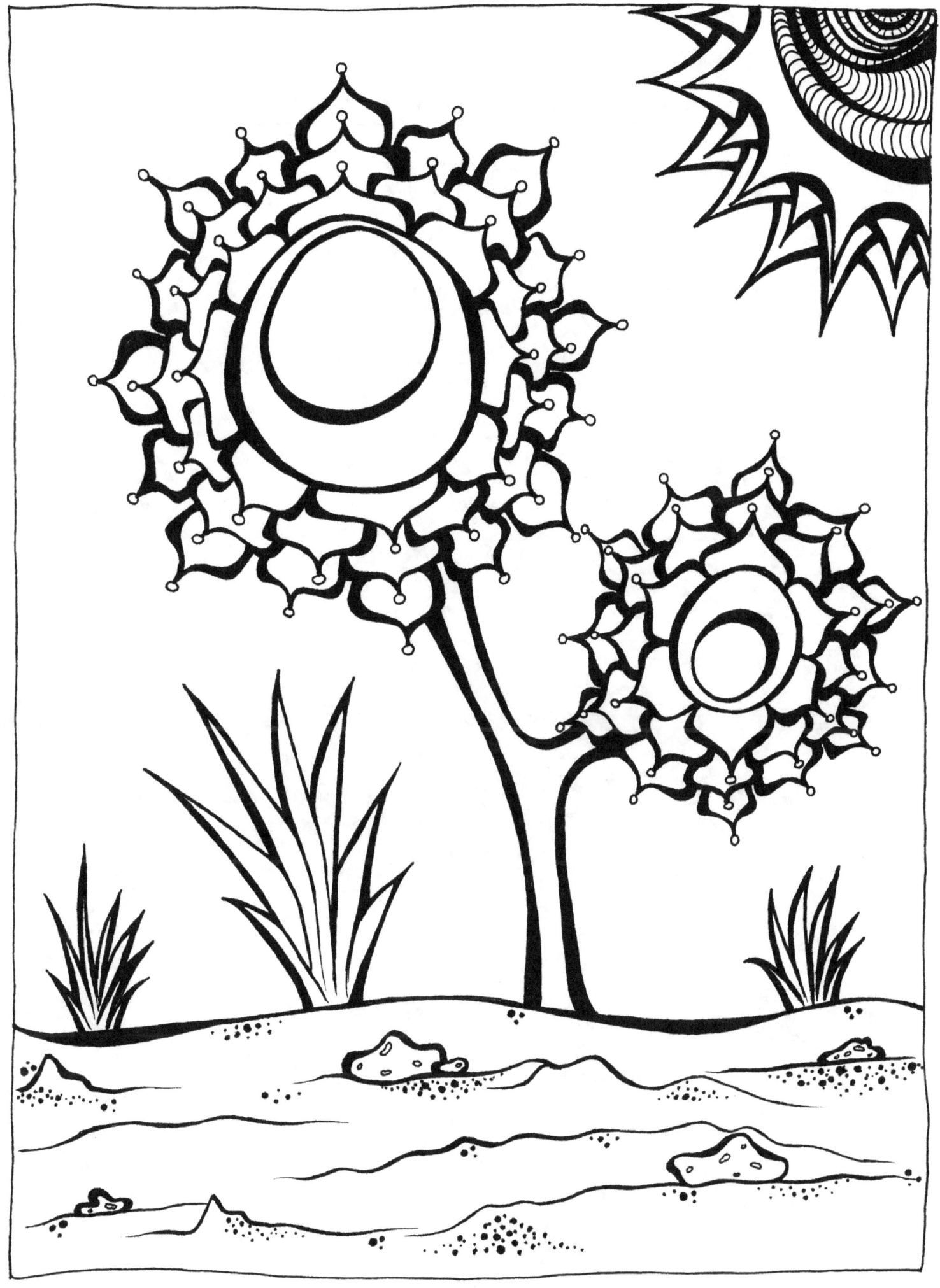

SarahMe Doodles Spring

Colored By: _____

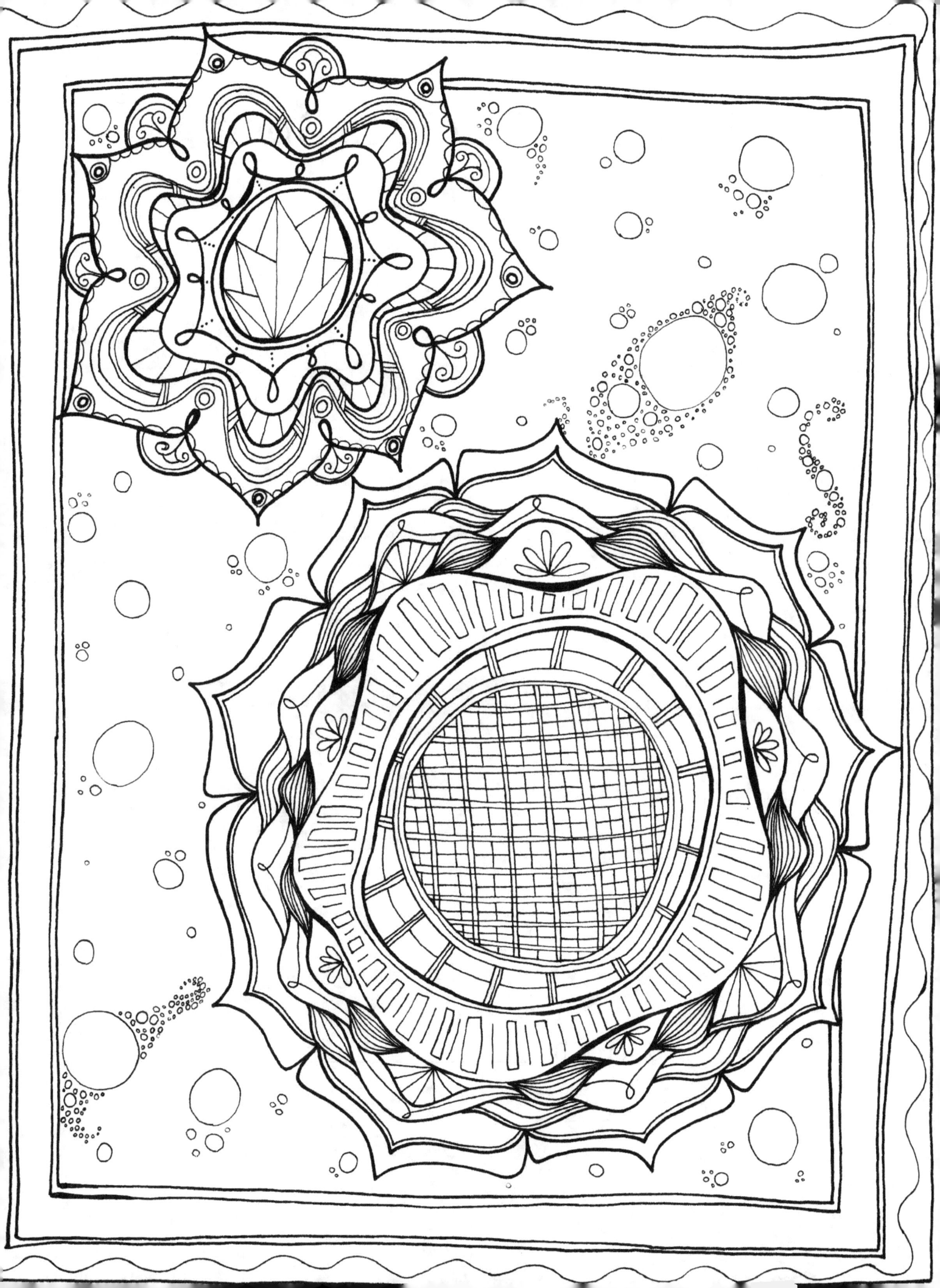

SarahMe Doodles Spring

Colored By: _____

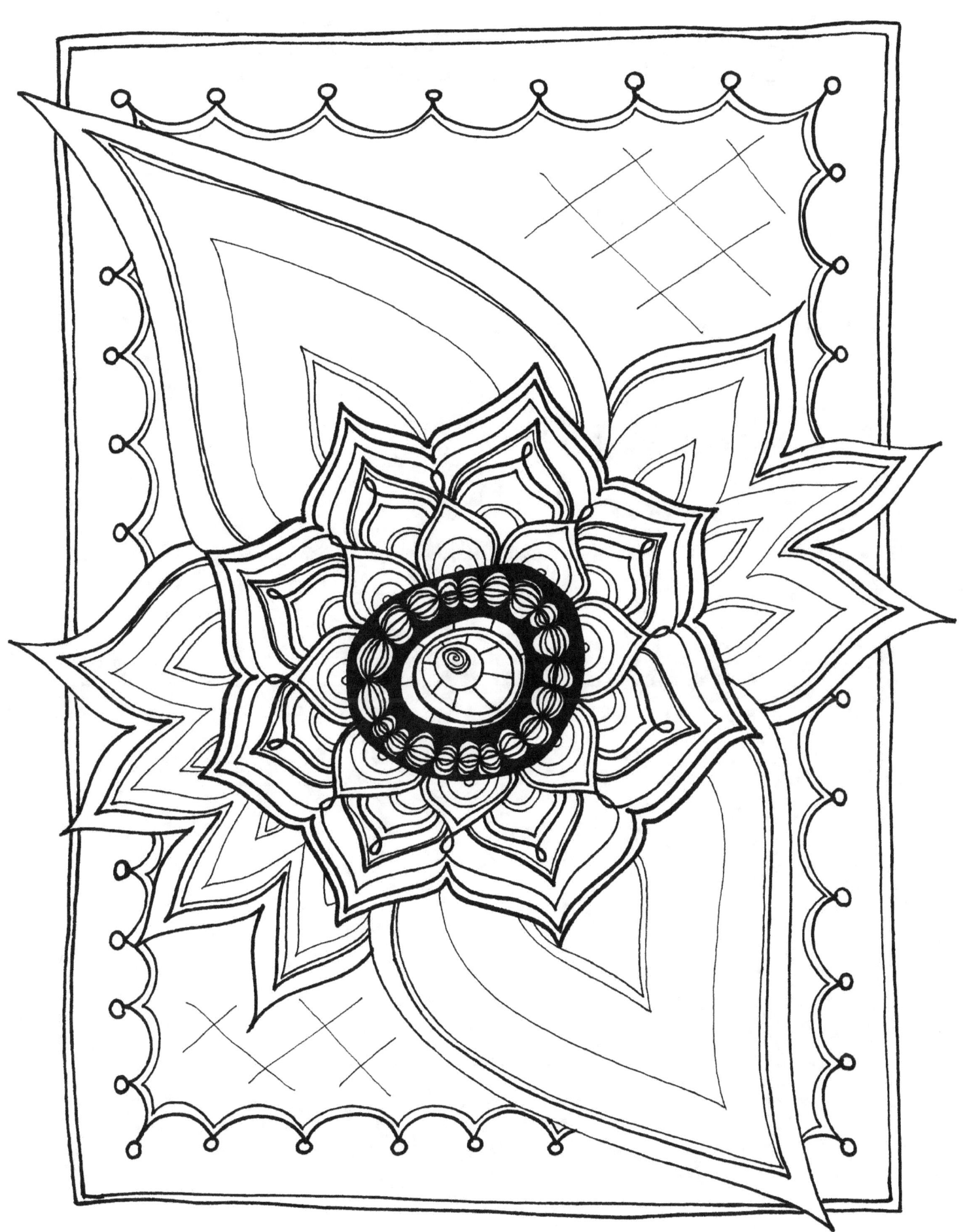

SarahMe Doodles Spring

Colored By: _____

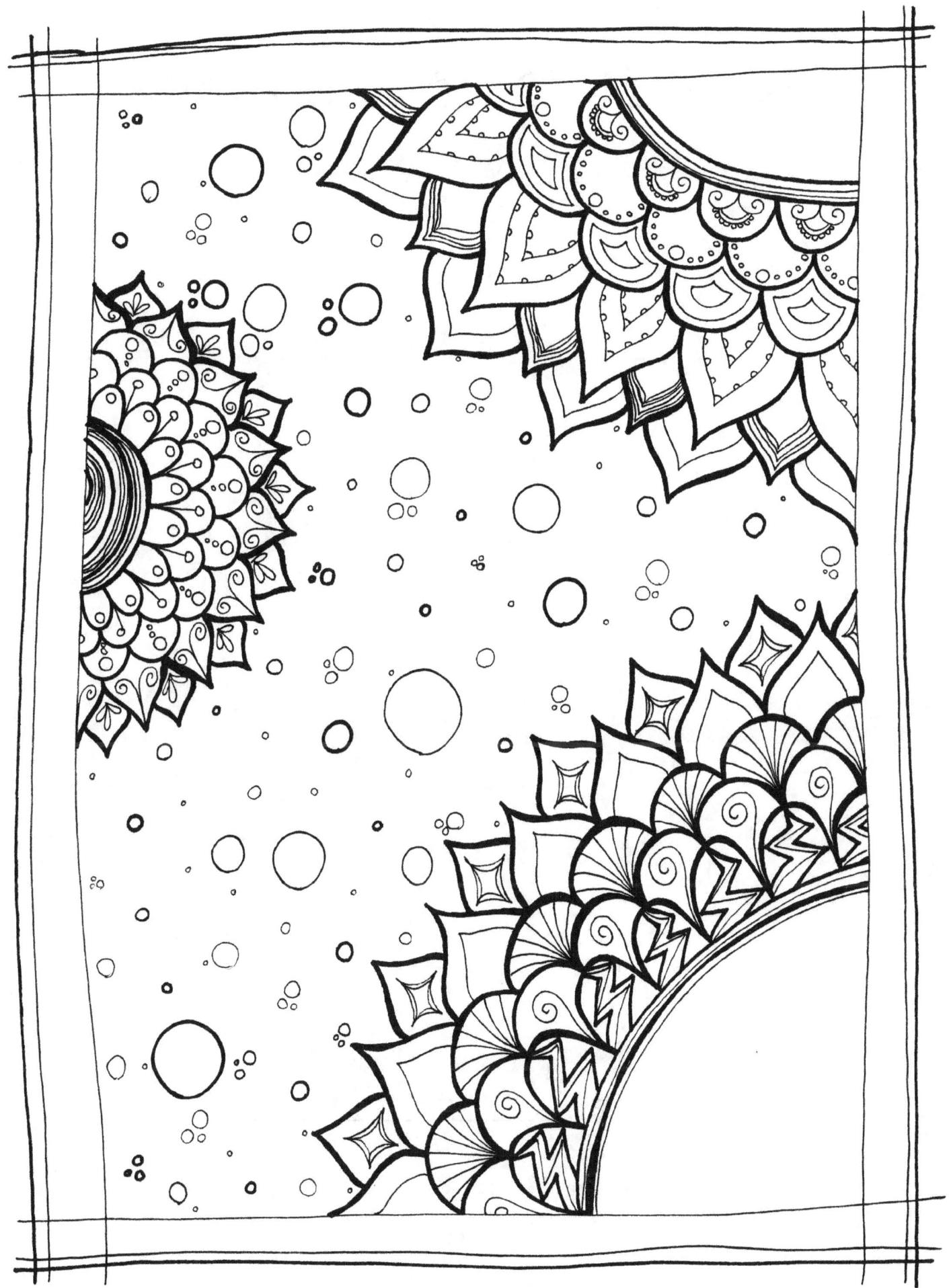

SarahMe Doodles Spring

Colored By: _____

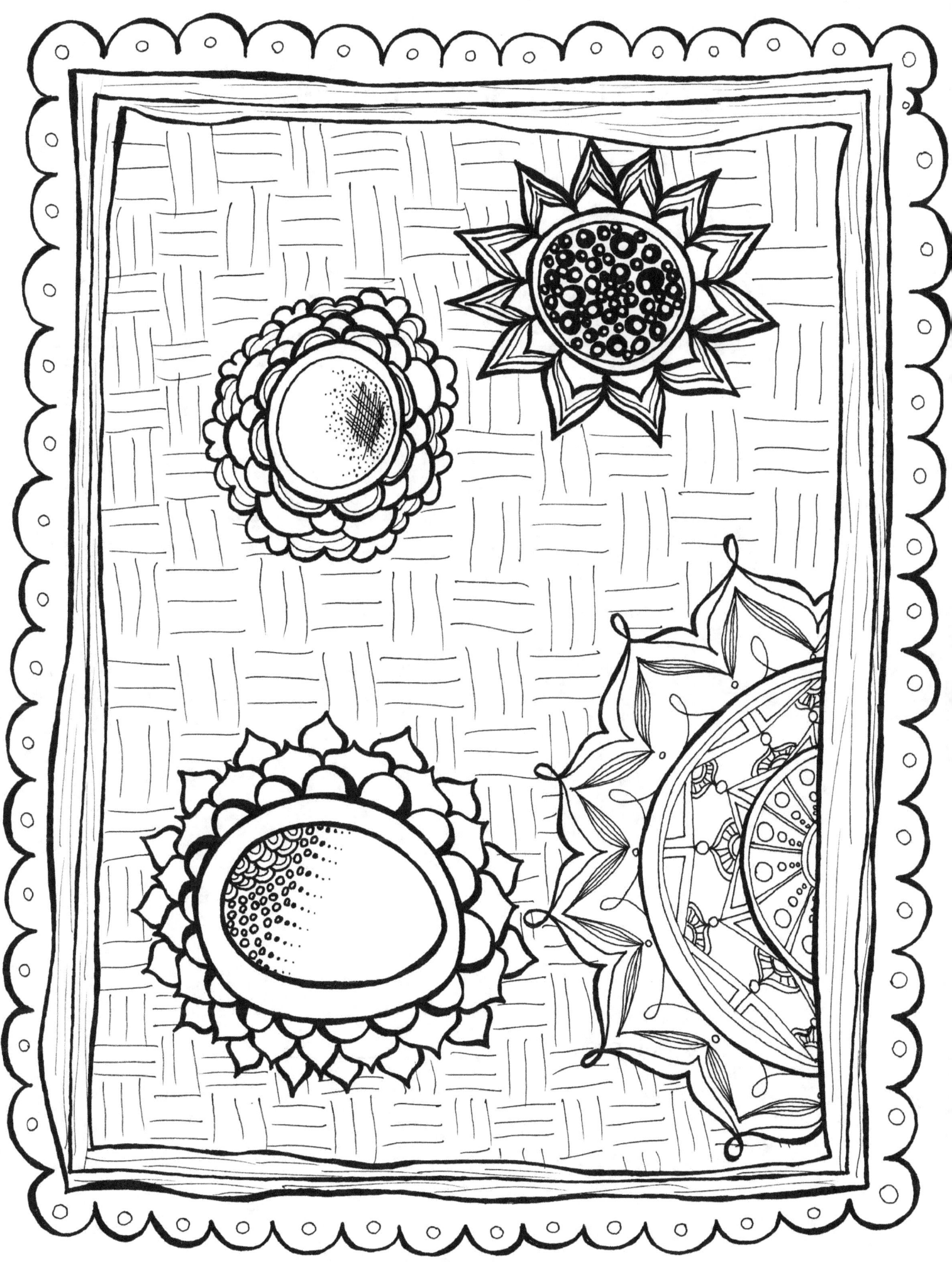

SarahMe Doodles Spring

Colored By: _____

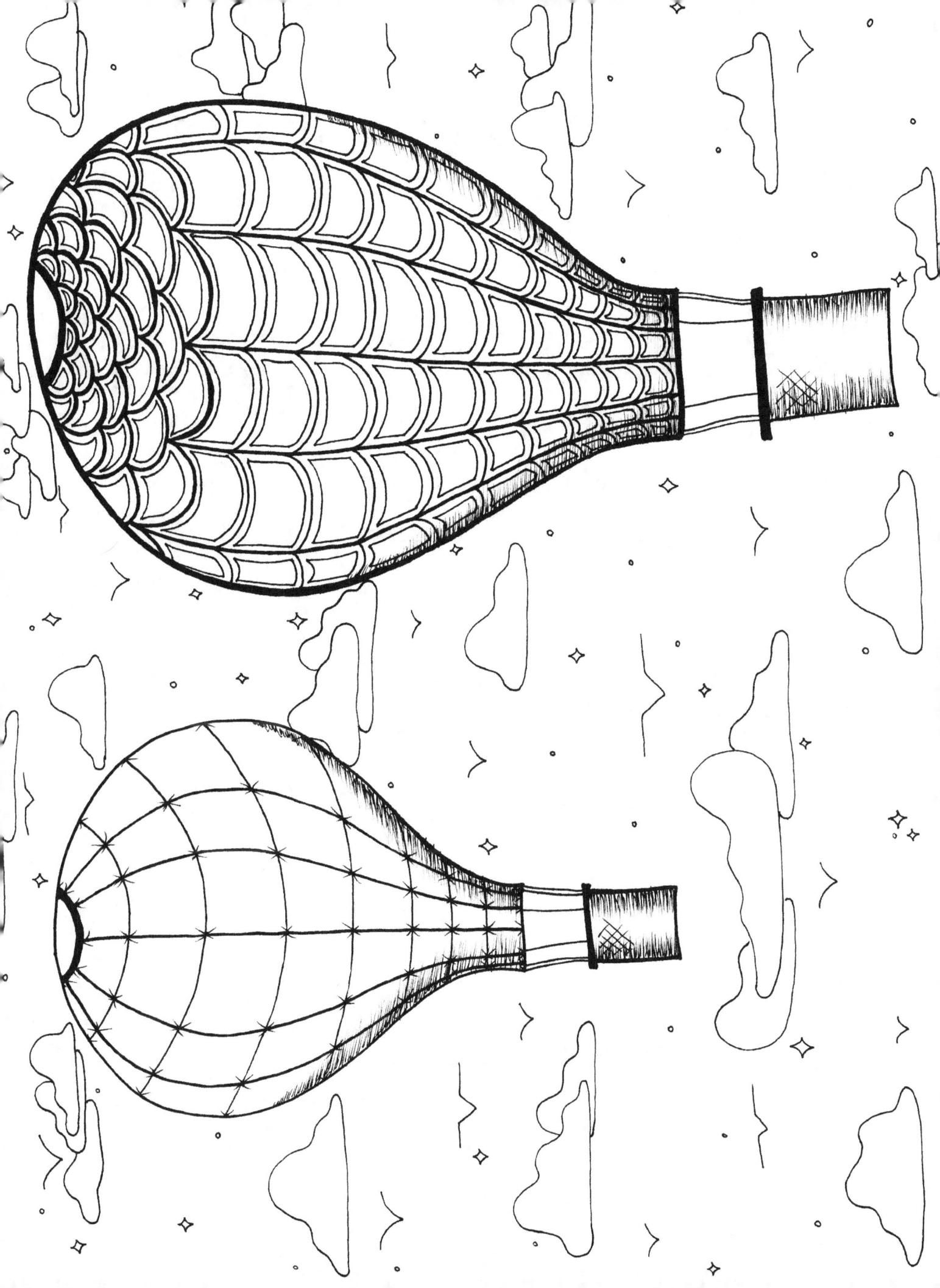

SarahMe Doodles Spring

Colored By: _____

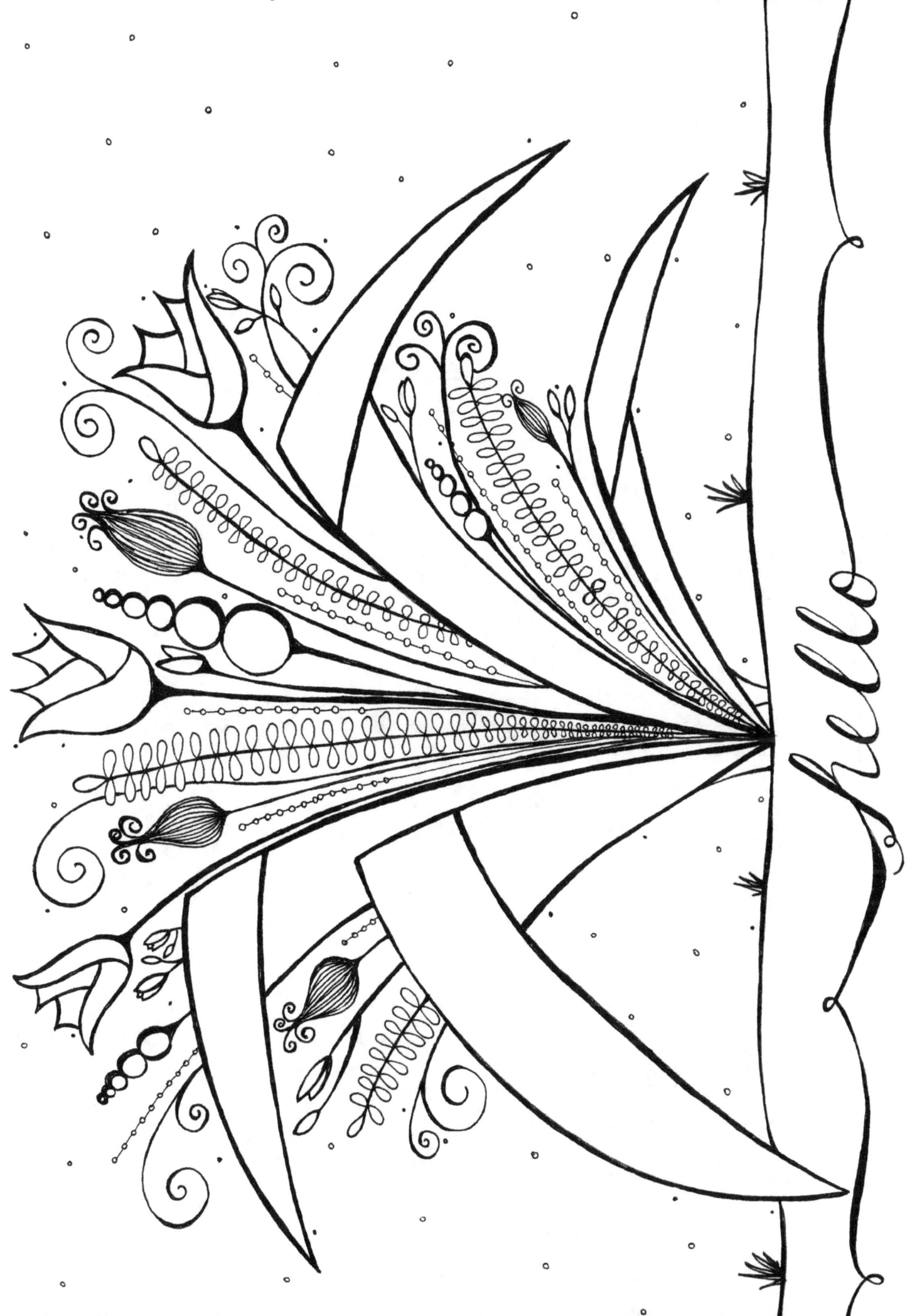

SarahMe Doodles Spring

Colored By: _____

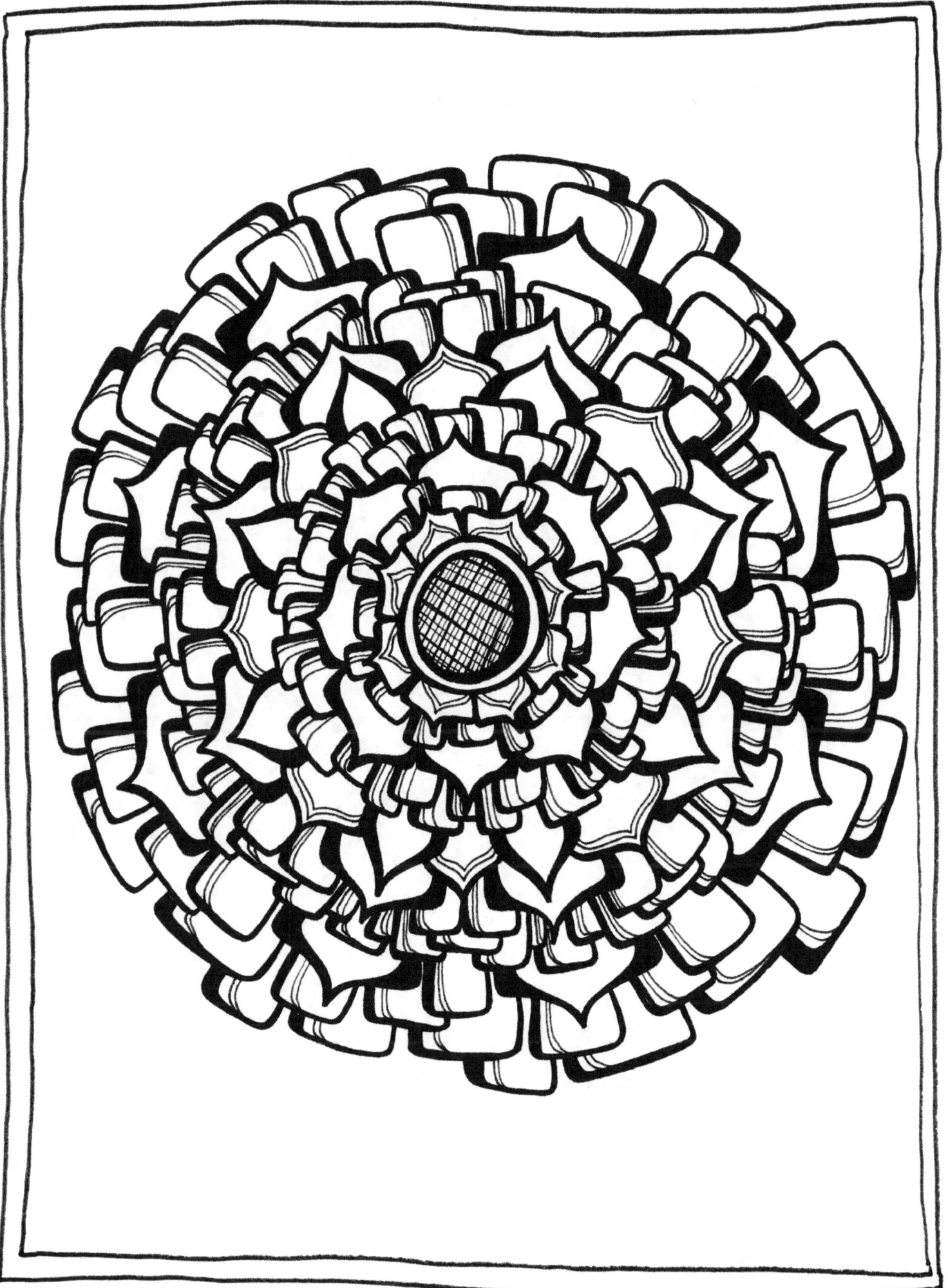

SarahMe Doodles Spring

Colored By: _____

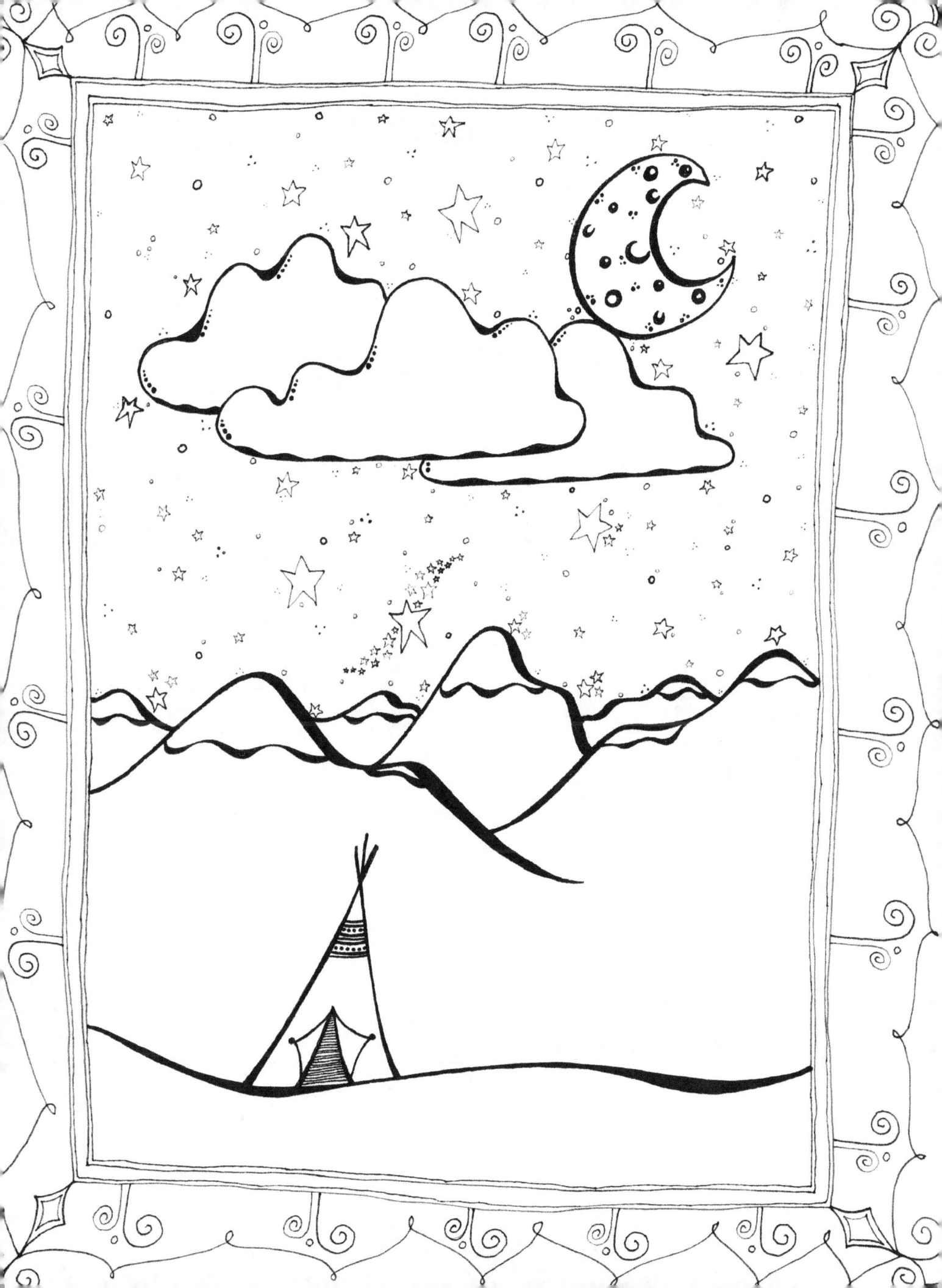

SarahMe Doodles Spring

Colored By: _____

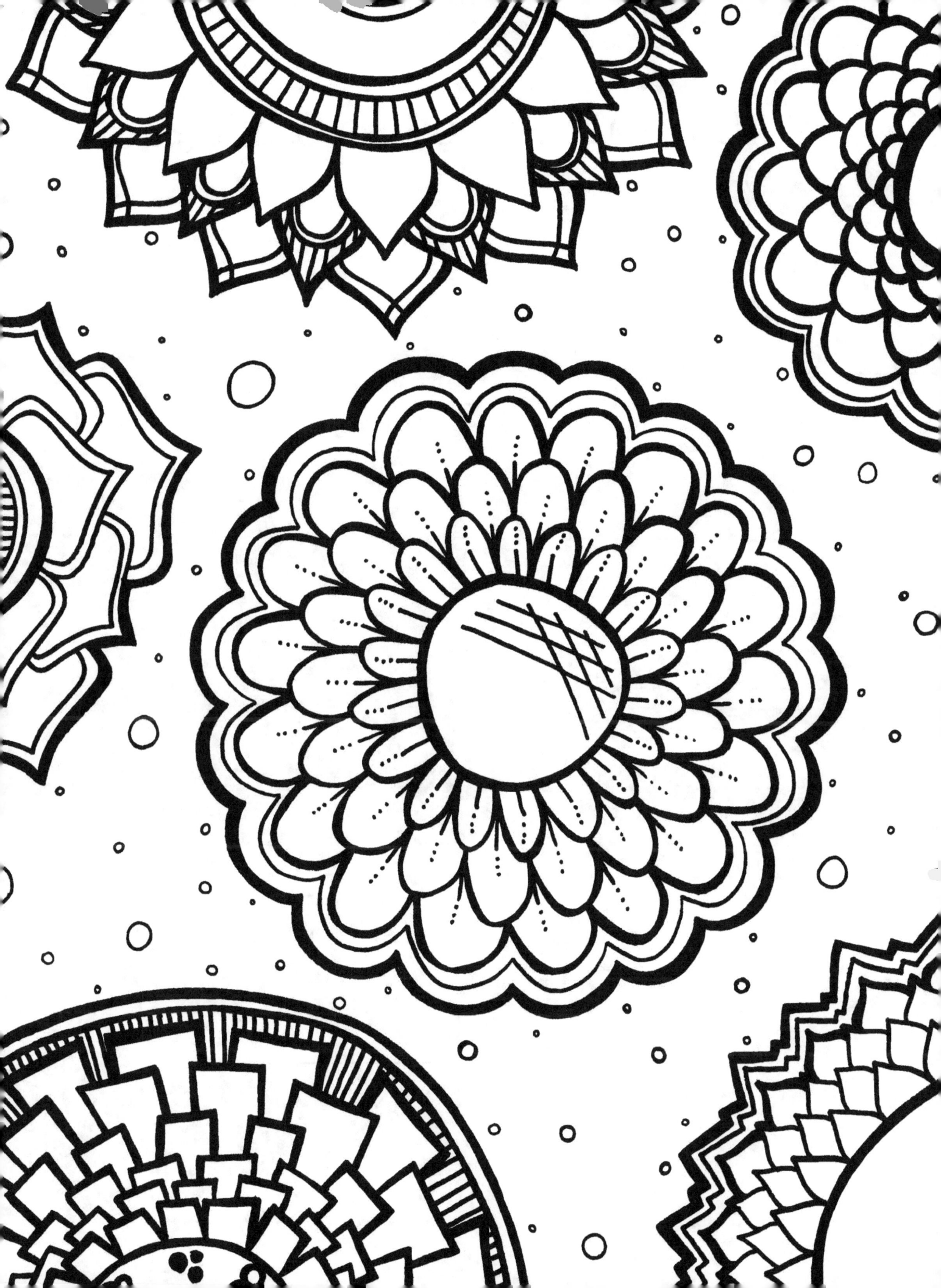

SarahMe Doodles Spring

Colored By: _____

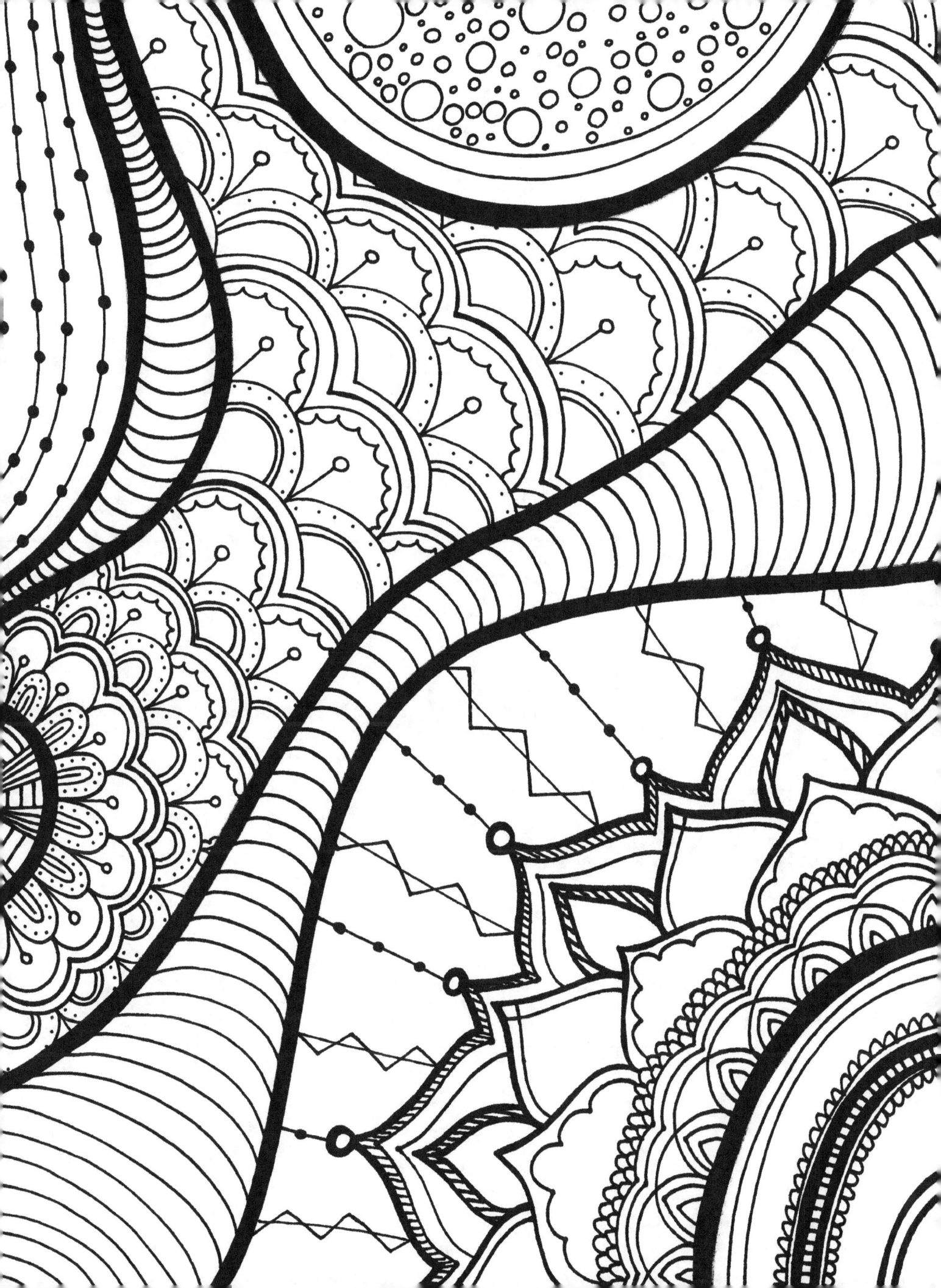

SarahMe Doodles Spring

Colored By: _____

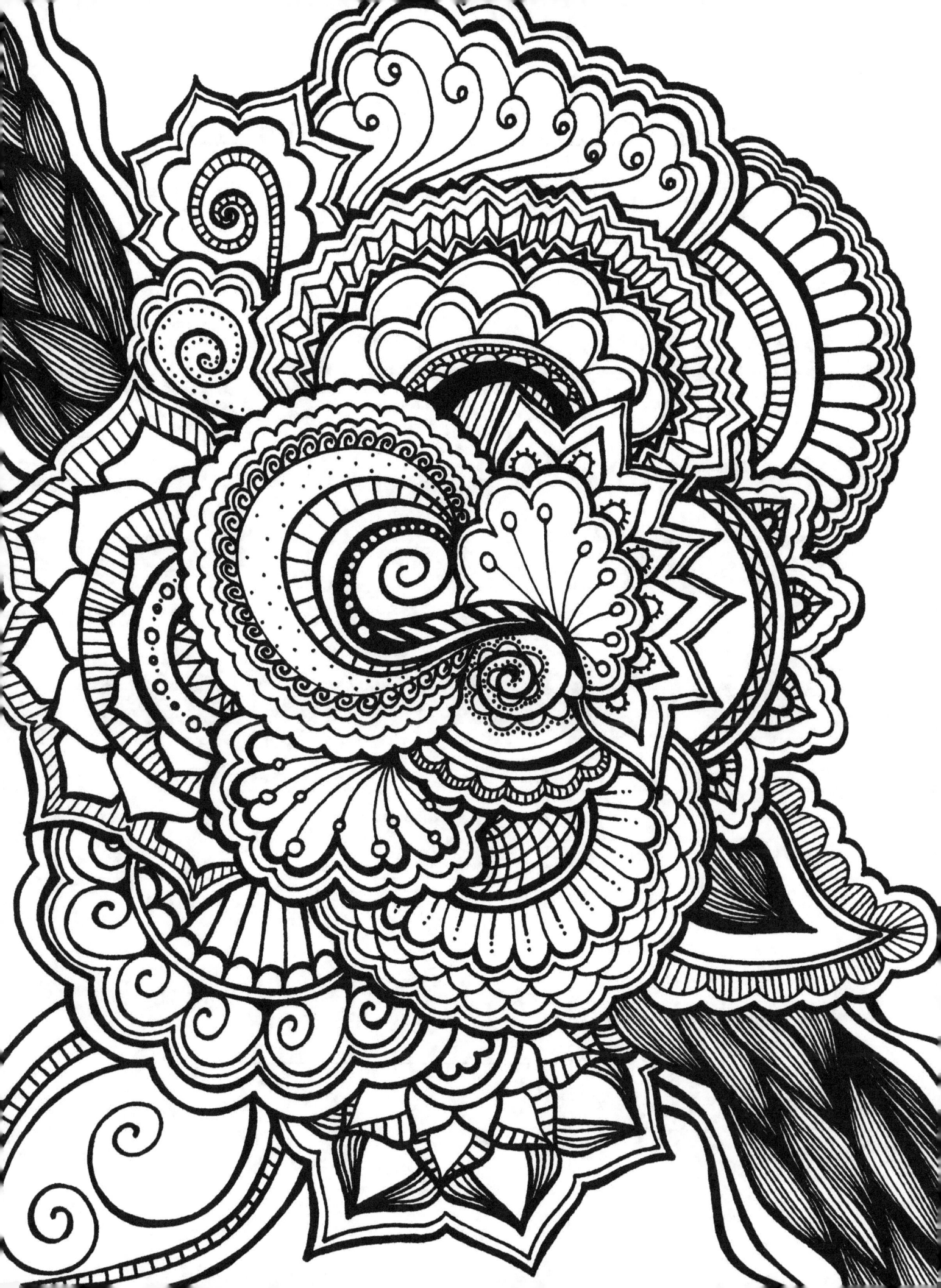

SarahMe Doodles Spring

Colored By: _____

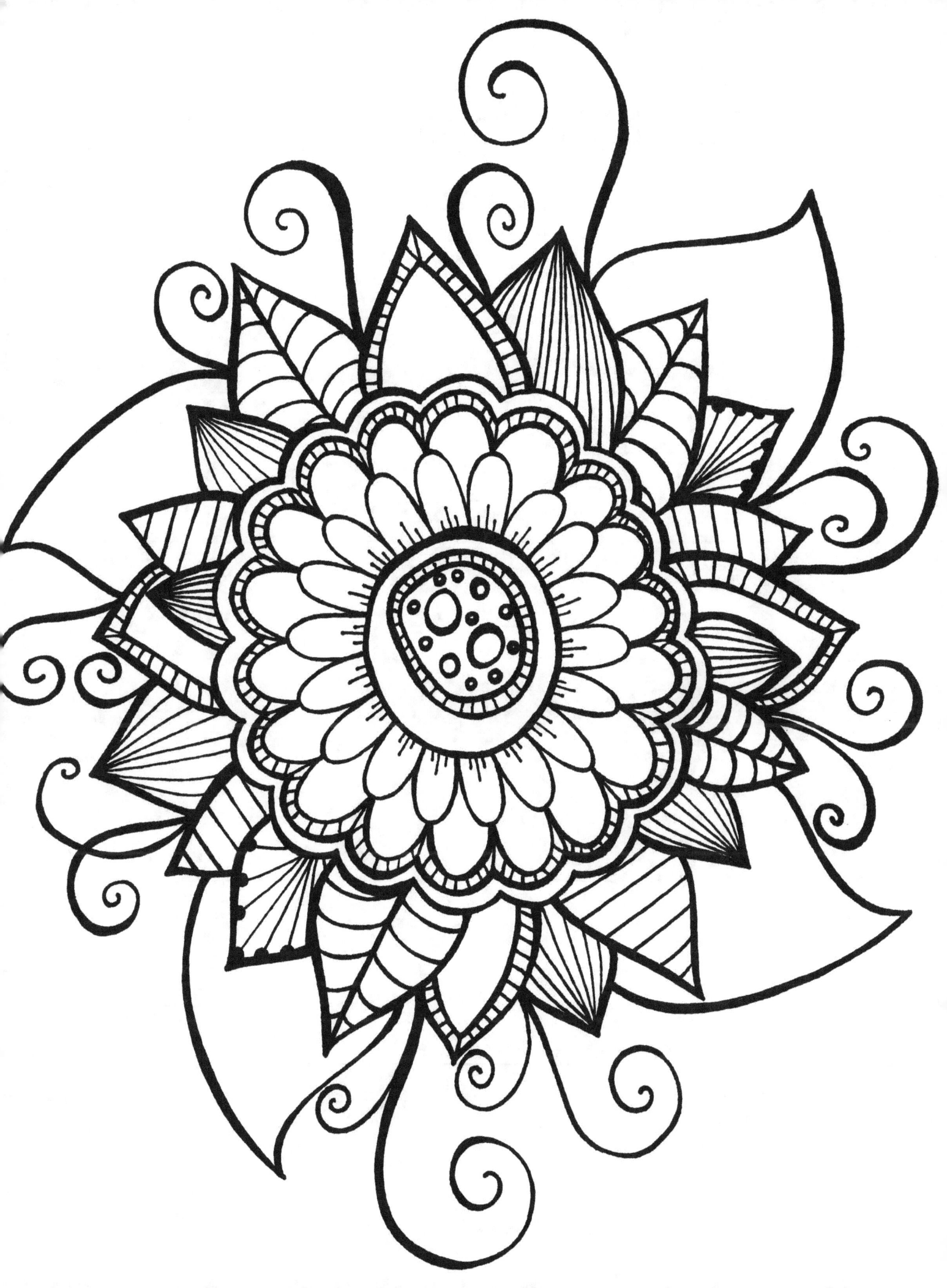

SarahMe Doodles Spring

Colored By: _____

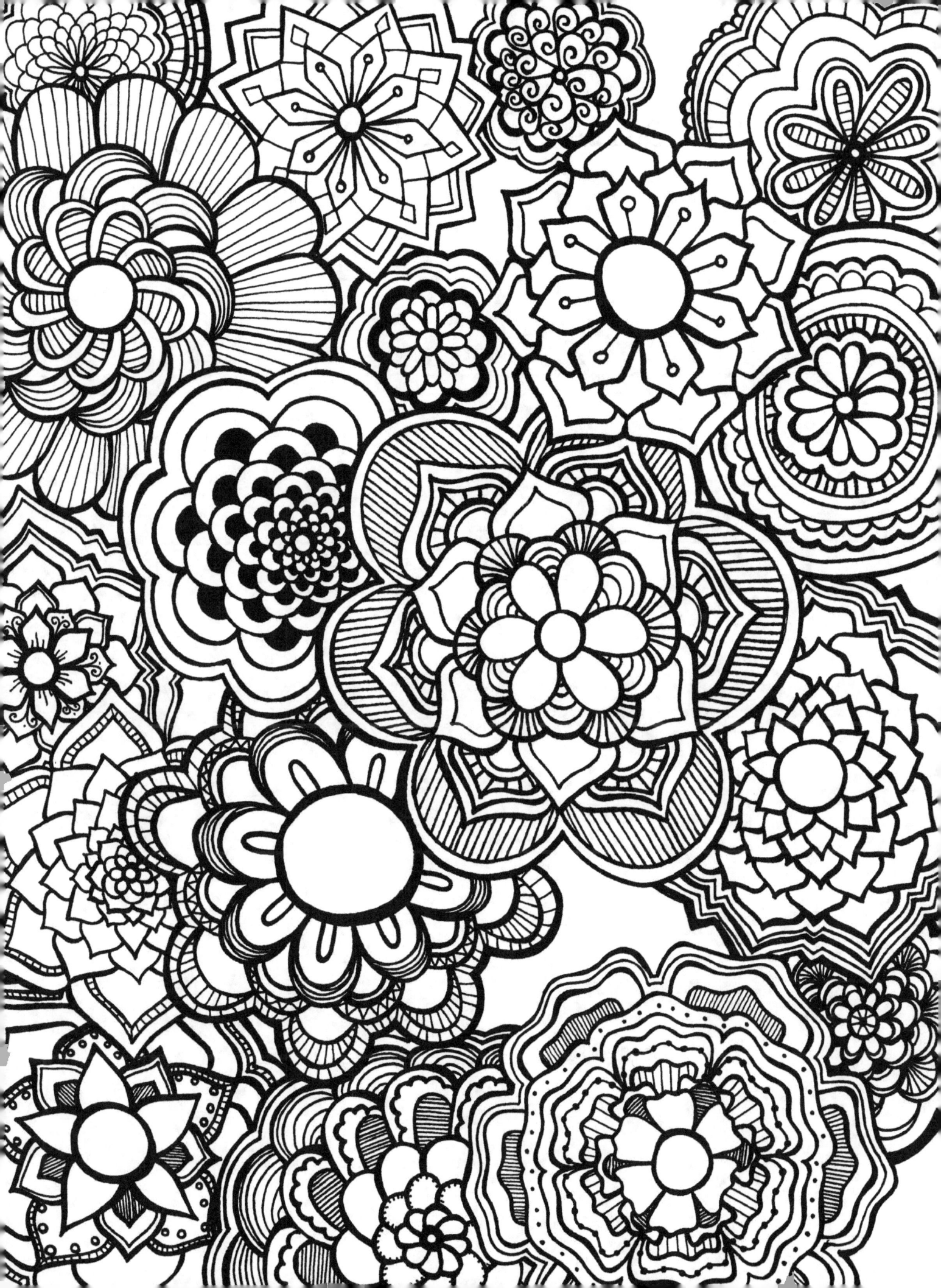

SarahMe Doodles Spring

Colored By: _____

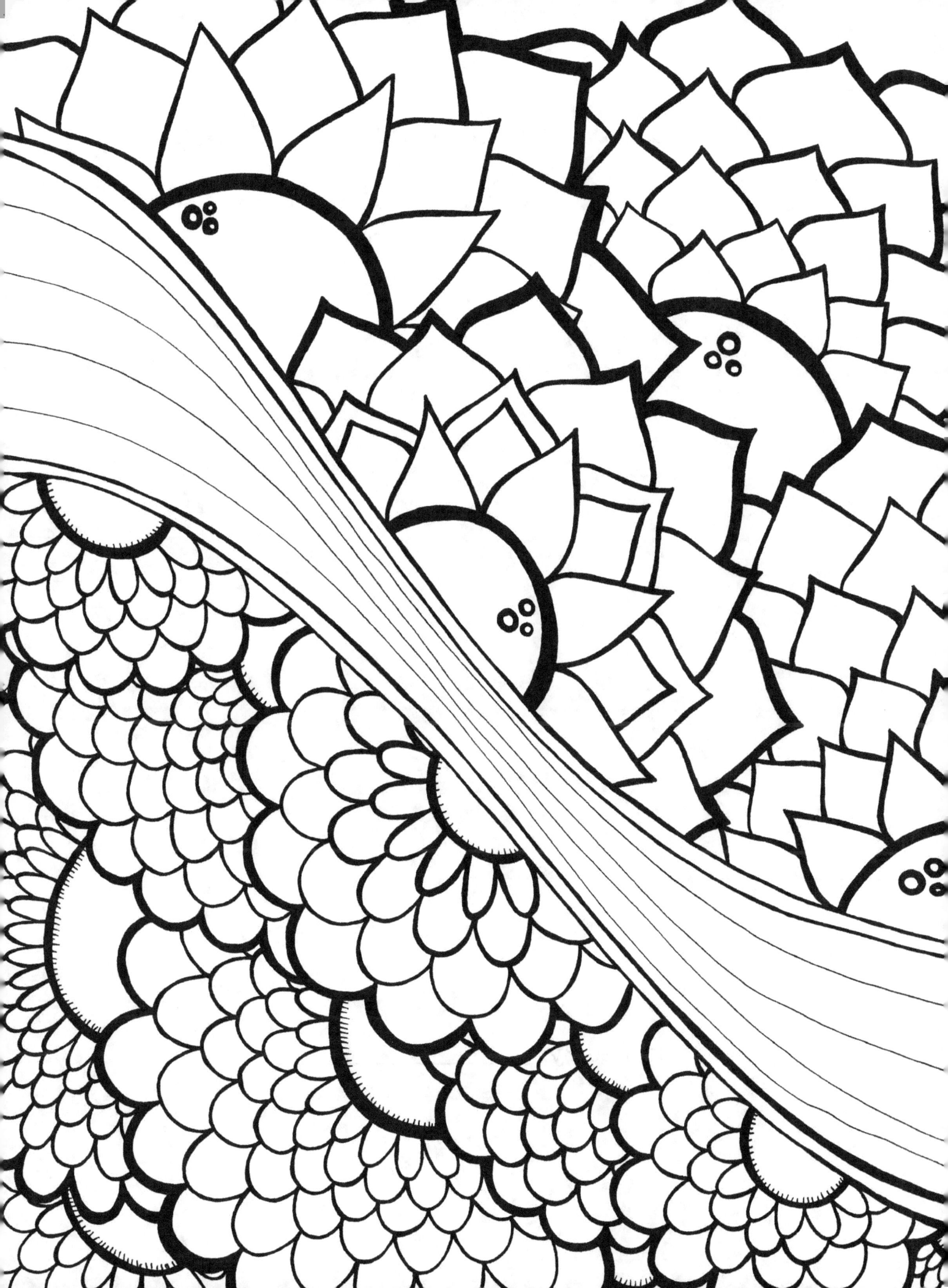

SarahMe Doodles Spring

Colored By: _____

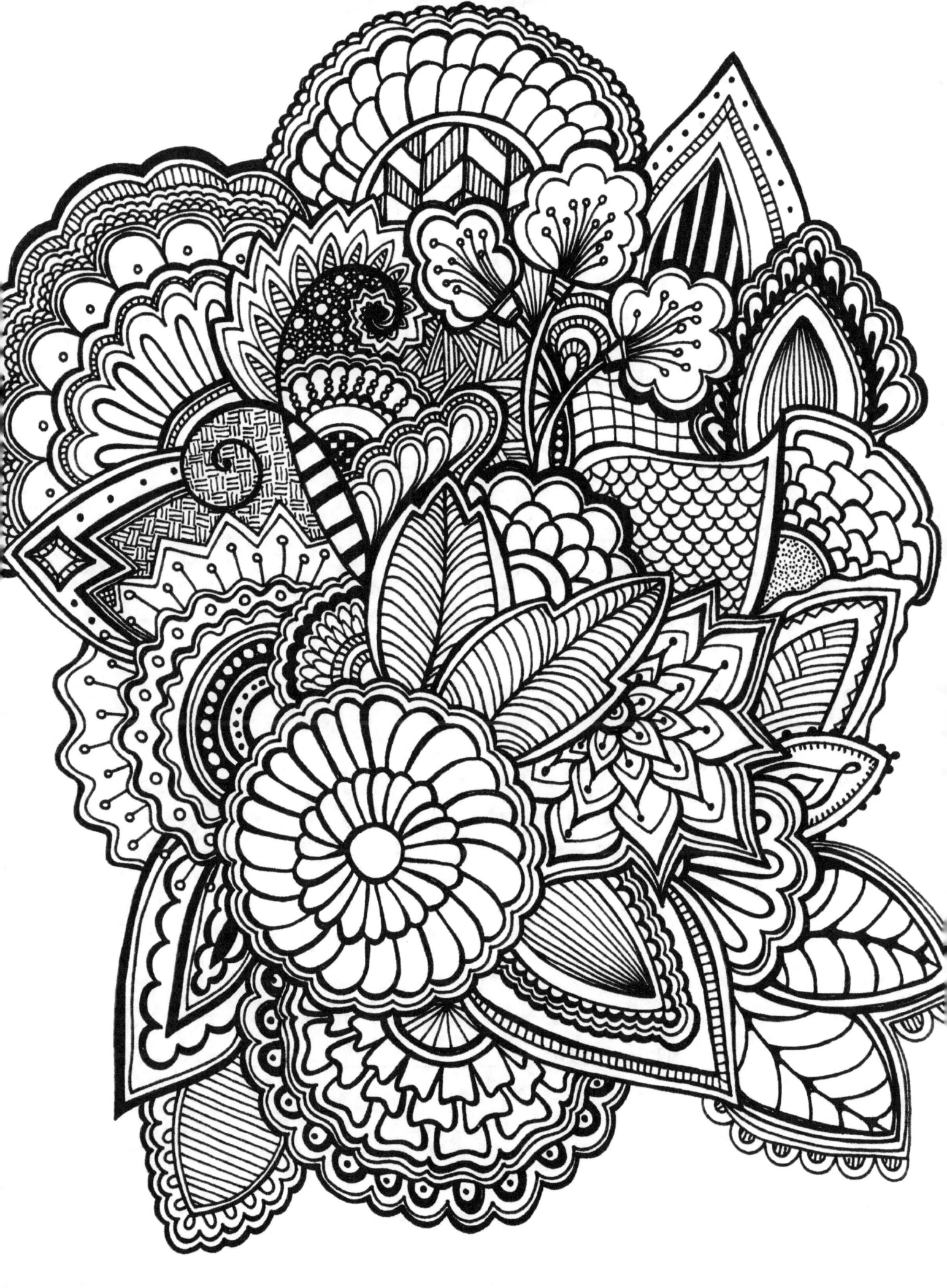

SarahMe Doodles Spring

Colored By: _____

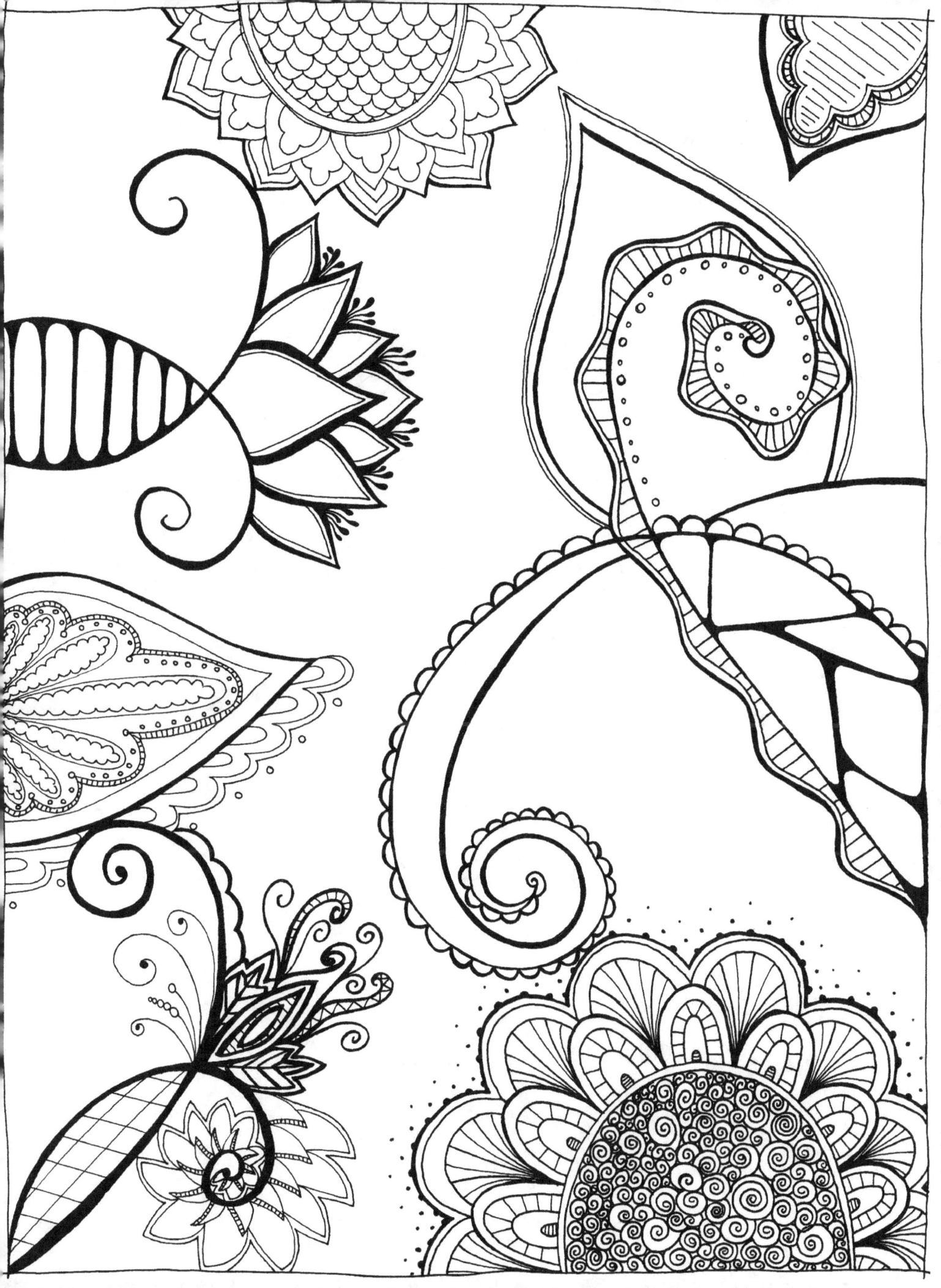

SarahMe Doodles Spring

Colored By: _____

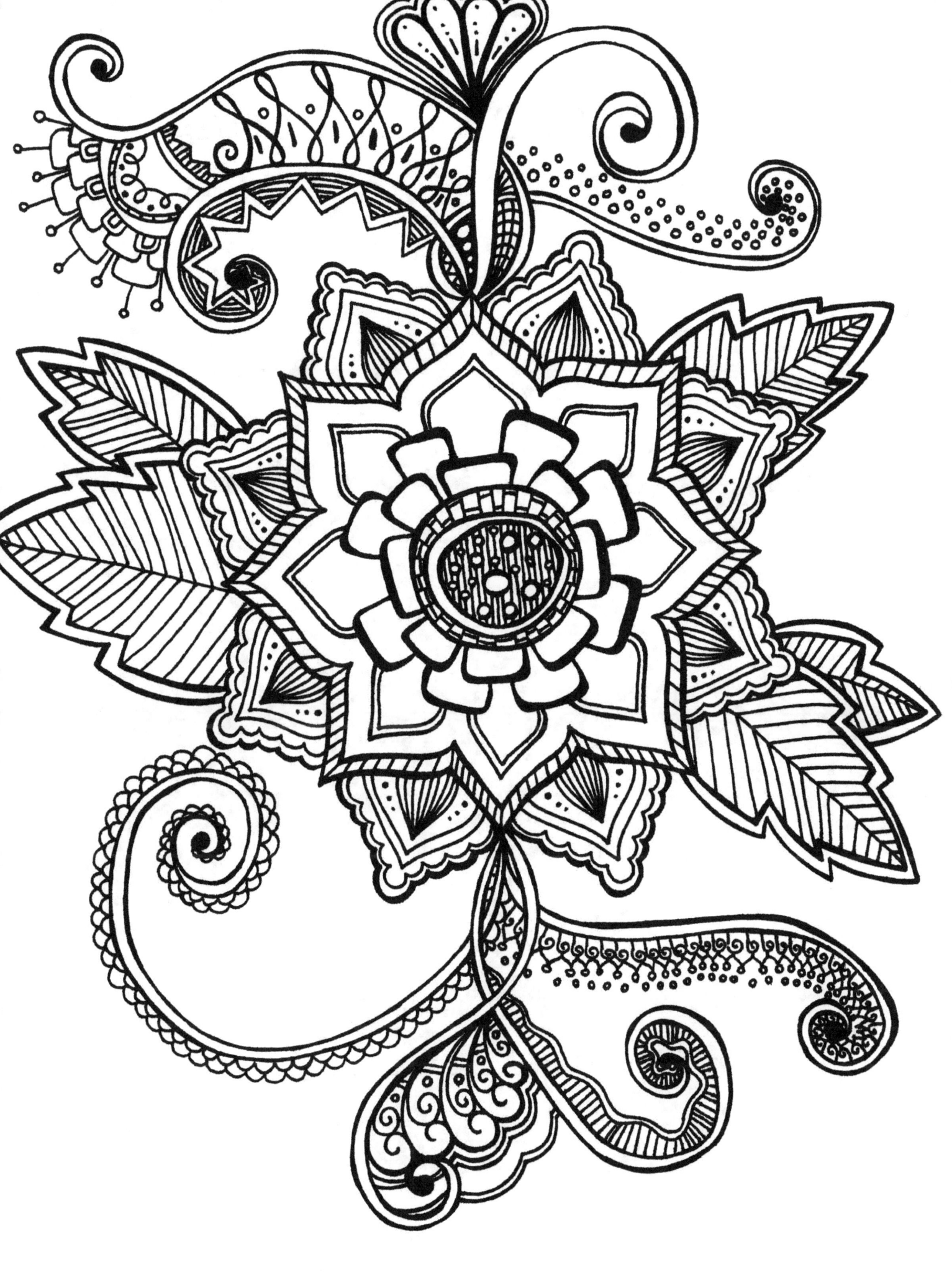

SarahMe Doodles Spring

Colored By: _____

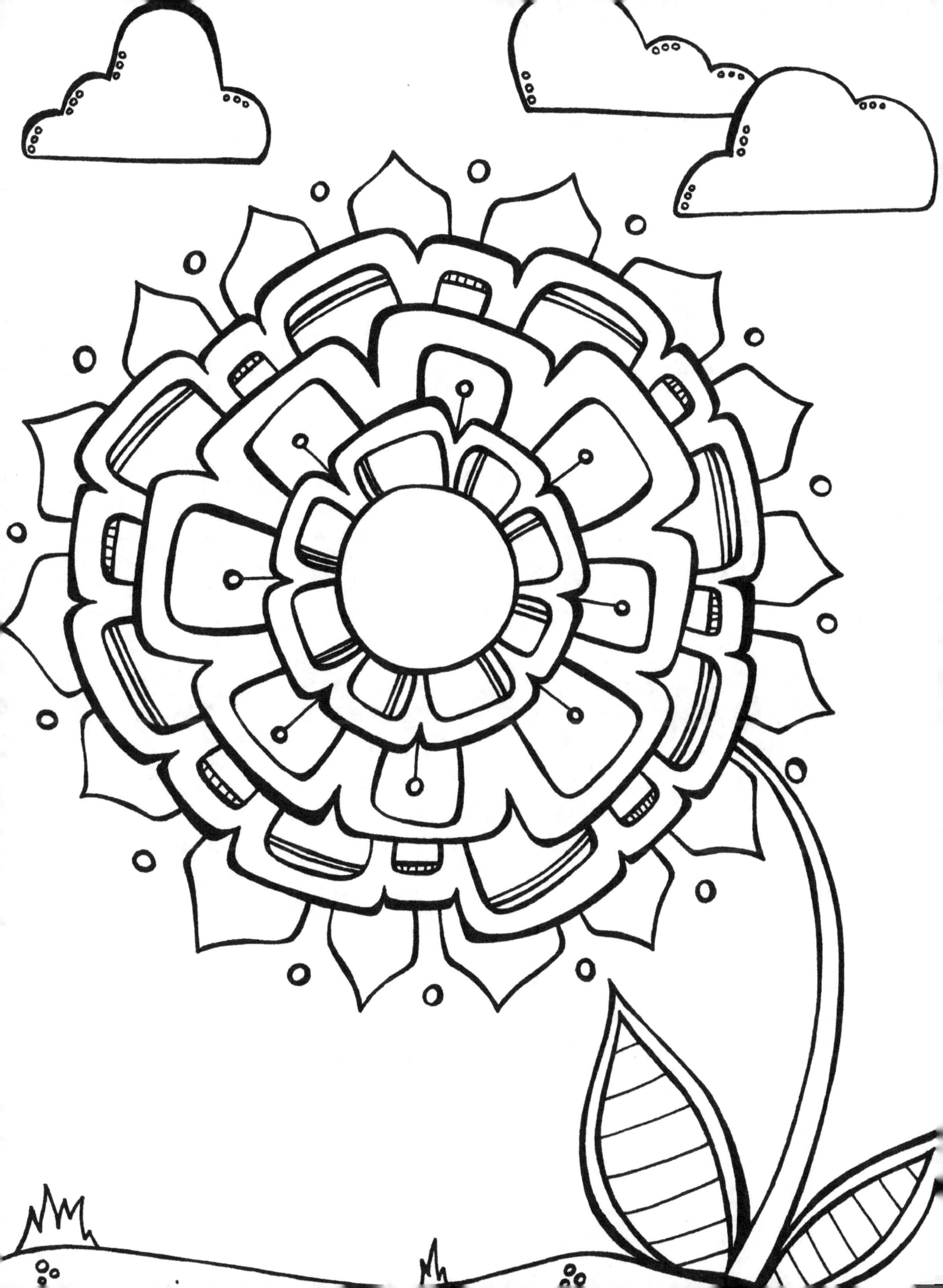

SarahMe Doodles Spring

Colored By: _____

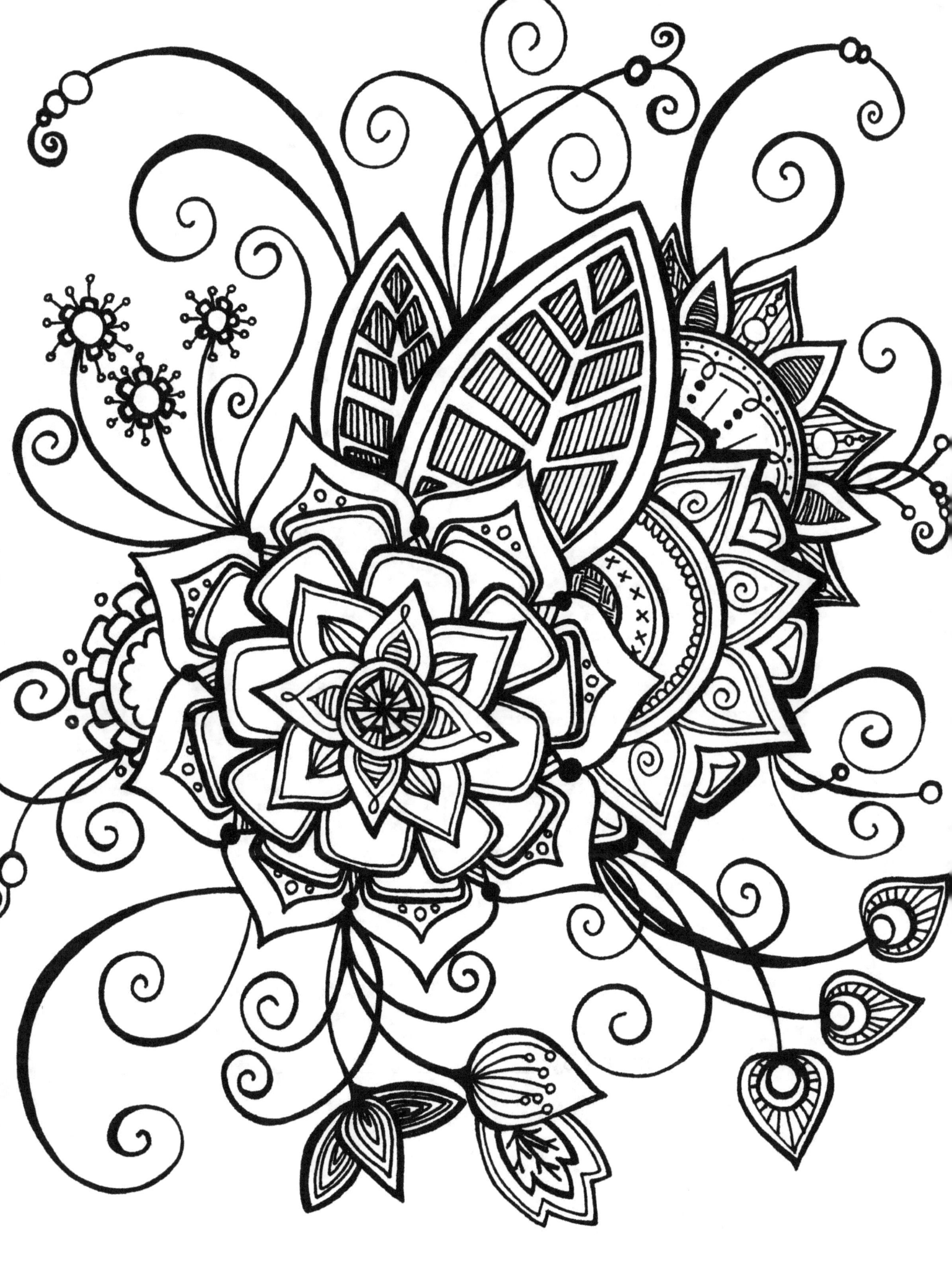

SarahMe Doodles Spring

Colored By: _____

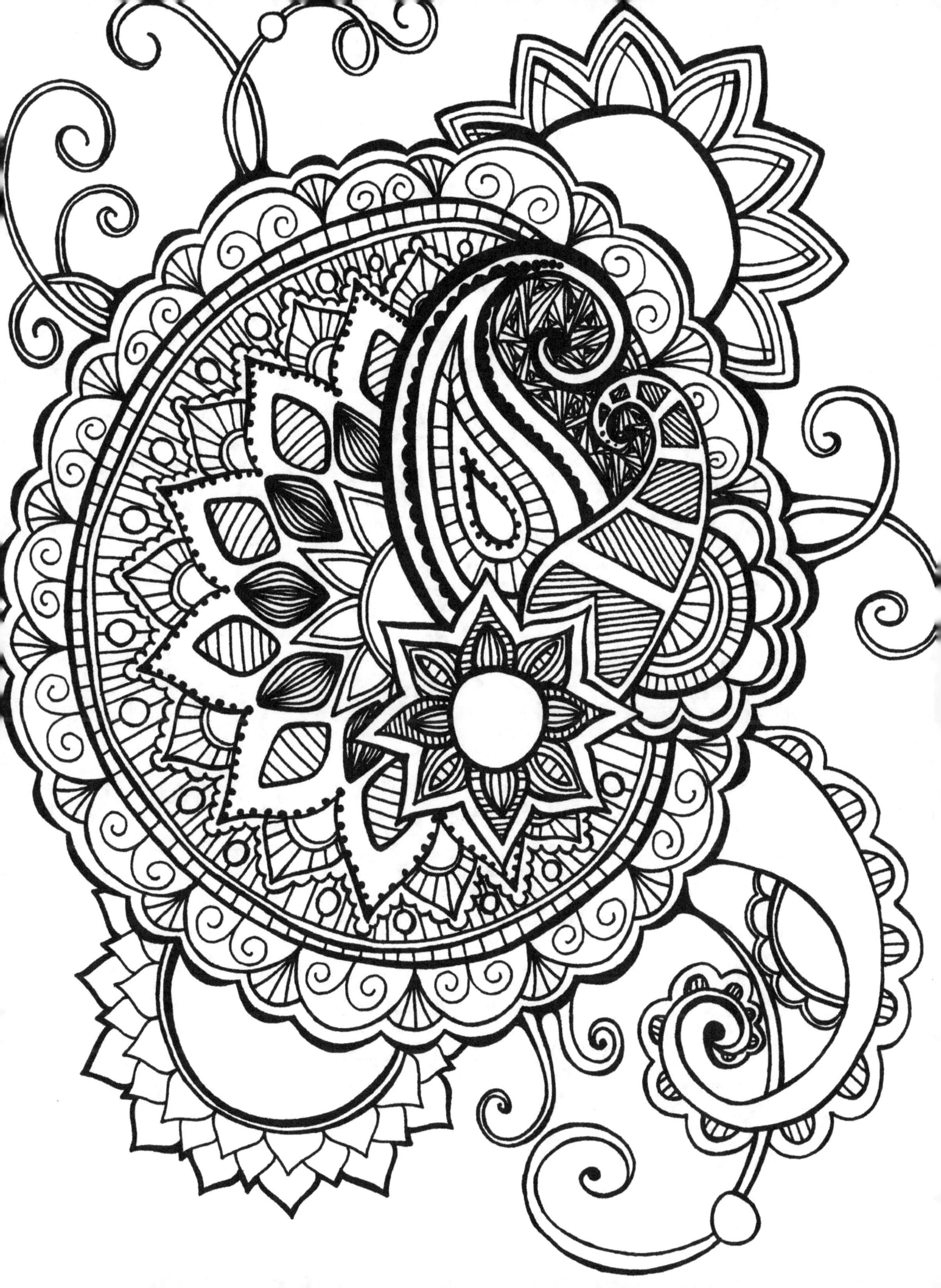

SarahMe Doodles Spring

Colored By: _____

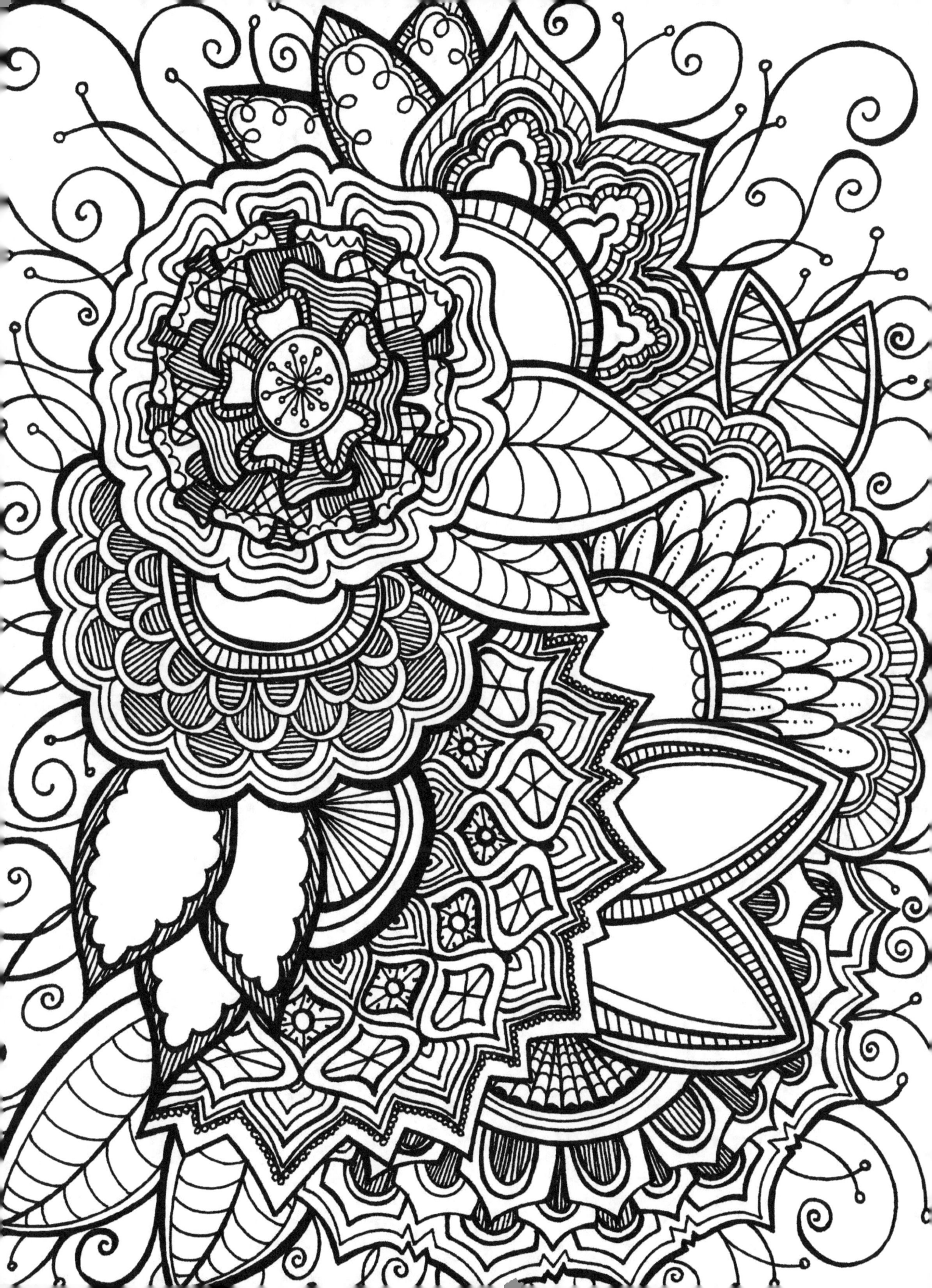

SarahMe Doodles Spring

Colored By: _____

www.ingramcontent.com/pod-product-compliance
Lightning Source LLC
Chambersburg PA
CBHW081739170526
45167CB00009B/3876